HOW TO SHOW
Kindness
THROUGH
Hospitality

HELEN ROGERS

Seasons Of Life

Table of Contents

Table of Contents

Protocol for the HealthCare Community

Table of Contents

Table of Contents

Final Earthly Planning

Table of Contents

Table of Contents

Table of Contents

Preface

When you think of the word ***hospitality***, did you consider the home, the business world, healthcare communities, final earthly planning, and the grieving process? Through the pages of **How To Show Kindness Through Hospitality,** you will learn how to connect and not perfect those we come in contact with. It shows how to build a friendly, generous, and loving relationship with family, friends, and strangers of every culture and generation.

We start with the family because that is where we spend most of our time and learn how to show love in countless situations. Sharing from the heart will foster our generosity, patience, and love. How many times have you desired to entertain or show kindness to others, and decided against it; reflecting on the fear of the unknown?

Would you say our knowledge of the task at hand, and the source of information will have a significant impact on the final outcome? We must heighten our awareness of what is appropriate in a given situation, regardless of the economic, social, educational or religious status of those we desire to serve. Through the pages of this book you will discover how to decrease if not eliminate reasons to NOT serve others with confidence.

You will find topics about entertaining unexpected guess with ease and celebrating special events on a budget. Have you wondered if you were leaving the proper tip for the concierge? Not only do we address the concierge but everyone that assist you in a personal or professional way home and abroad.

Does the possibility of making a social blunder or giving the wrong hostess gift concerns you? Keep reading your answers are covered including a section with Q & A.

As our families are maturing, there are times when the hospital and or healthcare facility will become a part of our lives. Chapters are covering both areas including how to serve as a caregiver or volunteer.

All of us have a season of life according to King Solomon, and our final earthly planning and the grieving process are times most of us find uncomfortable to talk about. This will increase your comfort level, proper protocol is outlined for you; including non-traditional services, cultural considerations, when to write your obituary, programs, music selections, and how to help the survivors of different ages with the grieving process.

Lined spaces are also included for your convenience to record your thoughts as you read the book. May your desires to serve others intensify, there is a blessing waiting for you.

"For I was hungry and you gave Me food;
I was thirsty and you gave Me drink;
I was a stranger and you took Me in;
I was naked and you clothed Me;
I was sick and you visited Me;
I was in prison and you came to Me.
And the King will answer and say to them,
Assuredly, I say to you, inasmuch as
you did it to one of the least of these
My brethren, you did it to Me.

Matthew 25:35-36, 40."

Entertaining
Home and Abroad

ENTERTAINING WITHOUT STRESS

Sharing a Meal

Casual socializing with friends and family in our homes should be both enjoyable and comfortable. The interaction among host and guest is congenial and relaxed in nature. The menu is simple yet delightful. Your guest(s) should not expect an elaborate meal especially considering you both work similar schedules. Formal events will require more preparation, and perhaps some outside assistance; such as catering.

Of course, the hostess should not allow her guest to convince her that the meal was less than appropriate for the occasion. The idea is to fellowship with others in our homes, so we must abstain from negative "they might think thoughts." "I'm grateful we can break bread together as friends;" in a pleasant, relaxed atmosphere is more important than the meal itself. So relax, and remember serving others in love is what matters, whether if it's fully appreciated or not.

Our desire to share with others should be heartfelt and focused. Pray for your guest (s) before they arrive. Consider this simple yet powerful request:

"Lord, I ask that you would bless our guest as they cross the threshold of our home. Let them experience your presence, comfort, and peace. If healing is needed, I ask that they receive it during their stay. If it's your will allow any emptiness in their lives to be filled. I ask that your love, joy, and peace be present. I thank you for providing for each guest— body, soul, and spirit, in Jesus name Amen."

Stress the Uninvited Guest

Undo stress diverts our joy of entertaining. Consider implementing these tips.

- Meditate and pray for guidance as you plan and prepare the event.

- Consider the purpose and social composition of the event, (who, what, why).

- Prepare your guest list and menu, considering each personality, and any special dietary restrictions, etc.

- Plan, your event with the entire family's schedule in mind.

- Don't create stress for yourself. If you need assistance or advice, ask.

- After you select the date, keep your schedule flexible surrounding the event.

- When requested to do other things, make sure they will fit into your schedule at that time. If not, be polite and say "unfortunately, I must decline at this time." Thanks for asking.

- Allow ample time in your schedule both before and following the event.

- Many of us have hosted functions or served on committees out of guilt, causing frustration for ourselves and misery for others. It's all right to say "No, thank you." After all, we are responsible for how we invest our precious time — aren't we?

- Sometimes we will rationalize and justify why we agree to do more than we are capable. We are responsible for stewardship of our time; as well as our other resources.

- Stress should be the exception and not the norm of one's life. When it becomes the standard remember that the unsettling spirit of stress will affect our health, attitude, energy level, as well as those close to us.

- Finalize your menu well in advance. The more elaborate the menu, the more time you will need to complete the planning process.

- Prepare a food and activity list with target dates and times.

- Check the on-hand inventory to eliminate duplicate purchases.

- It's time to shop — non-perishable items may be purchased on your regular shopping day; keep your pantry and freezer space in mind.

- It's prudent to prepare dishes ahead of time, when possible.

- Whether a dish is prepared today or yesterday is often a mind thing. Ask yourself, will it matter to the guest, when it was prepared?

- Set the table the night before to save time. You may also solicit the help of family. It may be necessary to have a light breakfast, to free up the dining table for the special meal later that day.

- Prepare a schedule and avoid interruptions while preparing the meal. Notify family and others who may call daily that you will be busy preparing a special meal; and, you will return their call later at a convenient time.

- Designate a ring code for emergency calls and remember, the answering system is also available for messages.

- This is the time when you will need to closely monitor your schedule. By the way, these tips could prove helpful in maintaining your daily schedule and not just for special events.

- Finish any final preparations early. Make sure the hot food items will have enough time in the oven, and yet hot at serving time.

- Use your last minute time to check any lingering details. Take a deep breath, and prepare for the guests without rushing, hopefully with time to spare.

- Do not panic. Perfection is not attainable or expected.

Compare what you just read with your current protocol and procedures. Keep what works and consider replacing what doesn't with this or simulator information. When making adjustments; always adapt them to your style and circumstances. ENJOY!

Unexpected Guest

You are attending an appointment with your spouse, and your phone rings. The conversation goes something like this — "Mom, a lady from Church, called and asked me to find you, and remind you that Missionary Jones will be bringing the guest from India to our house at 3:00 pm." You thank your daughter, and turn to your spouse and say, "Do you know anything about the guest from India coming to our house today?" Without speaking a word, his face tells the story, "I'm sorry, but I forgot to tell you."

STOP! Change what you are thinking, accept the fact that he failed to tell you about the visitor. After all, he is human. Instead, focus, and develop a plan of action. "Just add more water to the soup." To cancel your appointment after you are in the office could be costly. So you decide to keep it, but let the staff know of your emergency. While waiting to be called, work on rescheduling the rest of your day.

You knew the visitor would be dining with your family while visiting the Church, but were not advised of the date. You had a menu in mind already, along with a list of guests that would be joining you. On your way home, stop and pick up last minute items for the meal.

Once you are home, give each family member an assignment. Avoid creating a stressful atmosphere by rehashing what you "didn't know." Remember, a house has a spirit of its own. Yours is tranquility and kindness, so let's keep it that way. Most of our homes are not always guest ready, so you work your plan to get prepared, while creating a serene setting.

As humans, we must remember that when we accuse or question each other in a spirit of "how could you do this to me," we are ignoring that they are subject to forget. We must remember that these situations are a part of life, and must not be allowed to disrupt one's relationships.

Focus on what you must get done before your guest arrives. The solution is straightforward when we work together. You can start by preparing a simple yet delicious meal, perhaps with a festive centerpiece.

Use your best place setting, tablecloth, napkins, and stemware, with the focus on the atmosphere, not the food. At no time while the guest is present will you or anyone in the house mention that you had short notice of their arrival. At this point it is irrelevant, and would only make your guest feel uncomfortable being from a different culture.

Would you say our homes should be reasonably guest-ready at all times? After all, our families and friends will always appreciate a relaxing atmosphere just for themselves.

Everyone can be part of making and keeping the home life pleasant, and presentable. Consider creating a place for things. Show the family where and why it is essential to put items back in place after each use. When everyone know the guidelines and following them; that particular area will always have a tidy and organized appearance. Now expand this concept to your entire home, while visualizing the extra time you will have once the family sees the value of the change.

List some of the guidelines you have in place in your home, or start a wish list —

_____

_____

_____

_____

_____

_____

_____

SOCIAL EVENT BLUNDERS

Mistaken Identity

To call the bosses spouse by the wrong name, thinking it's the daughter or Mother; even worse mistake the son for the spouse — oops! When unsure of the relationship of the person, simply say, "pleased to meet you or happy to see you again." Let them lead the conversation. If you feel the need to say more, comment on the event in a positive way. You may also use this time to express that this event is an excellent way to meet family members and others from different departments that you otherwise would not see.

Never Appear Desperate

It would be best if you had somewhat of an agenda, do your homework by learning the names and interest of others that you have heard about from other sites, but never met. Don't be shy about introducing yourself to someone you are unfamiliar with. They will appreciate you taking the initiative.

Bringing a Non-employee to an Office Gathering

What do you Think —

The company party was at the end of the work shift last year; and one employee left work went to the babysitter, and brought a less than one-year-old to the party. So this year management decided not to invite that employee. The word got out, and it was stated clearly "no children." To not invite him without an explanation could result in an unfavorable employee relations situation. The employee should have been counseled privately rather than being ostracized.

Arrivals and Departures

If the party is in a private residence, note the time as you approach the neighborhood. If the time on the invitation is more than fifteen minutes away, slow your speed or find something else to do in the interim. Try to arrive slightly before or after the time indicated.

When the tone becomes more casual and one-on-one in nature, and you are not engaged in the conversation, it's time to leave. Also have a predetermined time to go even if you are the first to do so. After all, it's not a sleepover. Thank the host or hostess and quietly excuse yourself as you exit.

Not Controlling Your Liquid Intake

This oversight may cause your conversation or behavior to become less than professional. Ask yourself if you would like to be quoted or videotaped on what you said? If your answer is "yes," keep talking. If "no," change the subject or stop talking and listen. You never want your behavior to be break-room talk the next day. Neither do you want to be one of the agenda items during the staff meeting?

Uninvited Physical Contact

Could this be the time to make a change, or move to another area of the room? Do a self-check it might be best to call it a night? If your actions were prompted from your liquid intake and you are in no condition to drive, call a cab or ask for a ride with someone you trust. Keep in mind that it is okay to attend functions and not consume alcohol or substances that could impair your thinking.

Testimony of a successful professional in their own words:

"I attended MANY company parties and professional meetings...I never drank any alcohol...I did go to the bar and ask for a glass of coke or ginger ale BUT with no alcohol in it...I never wanted to be tipsy anywhere BUT especially at important events...and I never wanted to drive impaired."

Attending the Party Under Duress

There are certain events we are required to attend for professional and personal reasons. It is a serious mistake to allow our attitude to reveal just how uninterested we are. When we do we are defeating the purpose of being there.

My Story: *"During my Human Resource days, there were many events I did not wish to attend for various reasons; including the location, nature of the event and previous appointments. Nonetheless, my position dictated that I should be there. Upon my arrival I would share with a few key people then mingle with members from other departments, and quietly leave.*

If it were in a private home, I would mingle for a short time, express my thanks to the host or hostess and depart. You do not have to stay the entire time to fulfill your obligation, unless there is a formal purpose for the gathering.

Regardless of the venue always tell someone that you are leaving, eliminating concerns when your absence is noticed by the host or other guest."

Leaving at the Wrong Time or Saying the Wrong Thing

Never go before the highlights of the event are over; whether a presentation, special recognition or a state-of-the-business review.

Making statements about how bored you are or what else you could be doing in the presence of anyone may devalue your reputation as a dedicated employee. Others will wonder if you were sincere a few minutes earlier; when you expressed your appreciation for being part of such an excellent organization. Is it only for the financial benefits?

People may hear your words but they will feel your attitude
– John C. Maxwell

Adding to the Menu

A True Story

The supervisor was preparing all the food for the office party when one employee asked about the menu. They didn't agree with the selection and decided to make a dish of their own; and also instructed another employee to do the same, as if they were on the committee.

When they arrived with their personal dishes, the host graciously allowed them to place them on the serving station, with a smile.

When the invitation states that the food is provided, it is impolite to bring an item. It is both rude and inconsiderate; which could get your name removed from future guest list. To be asked to take their left-overs is a strong indication that the host did not wish to keep the left-overs. When the menu isn't to your liking, be a team player and try small portions.

If you are interested in helping merely ask if there is a food item that I may bring? When you ask the question, be prepared to invest whatever it may cost to make that item look as festive as possible. Also be prepared to accept "no thank you" as a reply.

If you feel that you must contribute, a modest house gift is always appropriate. However, it may or may not be served or used at that particular event. If you are good-natured about it, there will be other events where your contribution will be gladly used or displayed.

Eating From the Serving Station

It is impolite to taste test the food and then serve your plate. When the food is ready, you should go to the serving stations, get the proper utensils and proceed. If you arrive after the food is served and you see someone in line that you want to speak with it is acceptable. Ask permission from others then join your friend. The conversation should be brief, in a soft voice, and not interfere with the flow.

SOCIAL SETTING FREQUENTLY ASKED Q WITH A

Q. You receive an invitation to the annual office party what now?

A. First check your schedule and that of the family before sending your RSVP. If you are unable to attend, you should still RSVP indicating your intentions. Each reply is vital for the planning process of an event.

Q. How would a person choose the appropriate attire for the event?

A. There are several things to consider — what is the setting, who will be there, what do you want others to remember about you. Is this a time to promote a career move or simply to be comfortable?

Based on your answer you would select an outfit accordingly.

- Five Star Restaurant sit-down meal — suite and tie for the men, ladies basic black or navy blue with a touch of color or a trendy pants suit.

- The residences of the Manager or less formal setting — sports jacket without the tie or a fashionable sweater with matching shirt and trousers.

- Ladies nothing extremely revealing or form-fitting, your professional abilities should be the key factors.

Q. How much of my body art and piercing should be visible if I want to enhance my professional image or increase my upward mobility with the organization?

A. If the CEO was born since 1986, the company's culture is usually not a part of the suit or jacket generation. Body art may not be an issue. On the other hand, if a jacket is an active part of the office culture you should consider exposing the same areas as you would in the office; being mindful that you are representing the company during the social event. Our appearance reflects our personal judgment and consideration for others. Like it or not, others will form an opinion based upon the data you present verbally or in attire. "You can't un-ring the bell."

Q. Is a holiday event the time to wear cultural expressions? If yes, what should I consider?

A.   It may or may not be appropriate. Ask yourself the following — will I get the kind of attention I desire? Is this the first function that I have attended culturally? It will depend on the type of items ranging from a complete outfit to a simple accent piece. Do I want "look at me" attention or interesting conversation starters?

Q. My spouse/partner is not supportive of my career. Should I insist that they attend?

A. NO! Spending time with co-workers and friends should be enjoyable and relaxed. Therefore, you should not insist that they attend even if it may be expected. Their absence may raise questions, but simply offer his/her regrets. Don't allow it to spoil your time.

Story: One of my friends was offered a position at our corporate office out of state, and the spouse would not agree to go, so he was given a lateral position, and she went with him. As in the movie *"Mahogany," Billy Dee told Diana in his last plea for her to stay, "Success with no one to share it with is nothing."* It is better to preserve the relationship at the expense of not receiving the possible upward move; to accept the step and lose the relationship could be extremely hurtful and costly. These types of questions are best discussed in advance, as the relationship and career mature.

Q. How should you introduce your spouse/partner that no one knew about?

A. Approach the group with a smile of confidence. You control the conversation, and share what you feel comfortable with. Side note — also be careful when and how you introduce certain parts of your life.

My Experience: *"When I lived in Virginia, two female co-workers resigned and moved out of state. When they came back to visit, one had a masculine name, with attire that indicated changes had taken place. Since this was a group setting, we greeted each other and never mentioned the changes."*

Don't ask personal or awkward questions about situations that you already know the answer or even if you don't know the answer...awkward question should be addressed in private.

Q. What can my spouse do to make the best impression to support my professional journey?

A. Have a working knowledge of your past and current career as well as the names of some of your co-workers. Respectfully mingle with upper management as well as your peers. Dress the part of a responsible individual and capable life partner, be discrete, sociable and demonstrate a professional attitude.

Q. What do you say after calling a person by the wrong name?

A. Offer an immediate, sincere apology. Usually, it will be accepted as this is a common human frailty.

Q. What should one do if the boss or spouse/partner drink too much and become unprofessional?

A. *The boss* — if you know them well, guide them away from the group into a private area and talk with them. Ask a friend or colleague to assist you to avoid any misunderstandings. Guide the conversation toward getting them to admit that "they may not be feeling well, or perhaps too well." Ask if you can help, perhaps get their spouse. Do something constructive, after all this is a member of the workplace family.

The spouse or partner — "gently encourage them to change what they are drinking. Ask them to go for a walk or get some fresh air." Sometimes the bartender can help by recommending a different beverage. "Suggest that the person eat some food." Always remember that you can only suggest. It's the mindset of the individual as to the results.

My Story: *"I remember some time ago when the party was over a friend of ours was unable to drive themselves home safely; so a friend drove them. Because of the relationship, the event was not 'water cooler' conversation the next day."*

Q. You arrive at the party, greet the host and there are no seats available. Now what?

A. Ask the host for assistance or speak with the bartender while searching for a friendly face, or a   group to join. If it's a business function, include your department or location in your introduction. If they are seated, smile and say "may I join you?" Once seated, listen before you contribute to the conversation.

Q. There are several food stations in the room, and the person in front of you is eating from the containers while serving their plate. Is this proper?

A. No, it is inconsiderate and unsanitary to sample food from the serving station or line. If you are unsure of a particular food item, take a small serving, and if you like it, you may return for more.

Q. You gave your Supervisor what you believe to be an appropriate gift, and the water cooler talk is not positive. Do I ask the supervisor about it?

A. Consider the nature of the conversation and who said it. If it is the office gossip group, let it go. If the source is close to the recipient and knowledgeable of what is appropriate, consider asking them for suggestions before you shop the next time. Remember to approach them from an impartial point of interest, never mentioning that you are aware of their previous comment. Usually, a credible and considerate person will not gossip, but will approach you directly with their concern.

Q. What would you say are the most practical three gifts that virtually all managers would appreciate year round?

A. 1st Improved profits and productivity,
2nd Hire Employees Who Improve Profits and Productivity,
3rd Develop and Train your employees, so they become more Profitable and Productive — Michael Mercer, Ph.D. (drmercer@mercersystems.com)

Q. You are networking, and the person wants to talk business in detail, how do I disconnect without being rude?

A. Just say — "I would love to continue this conversation some other time." May I have your card? If they do not have a card ask them to write it on a napkin (if paper). Gently ask them to write it so you can read it, to say it and I will write it. You may turn your card over and hand it to them. Never appear anxious or offer to write it for them. You are now in the administrative role.

Yes, there is a fine line when it comes to getting the contact's info and appearing anxious. Then excuse yourself by turning to another person or group. The restroom is also a path of escape.

People will forget what you said, people will forget what you did, but people will never forget how you made them feel.
— Maya Angelou

Q. How do I prepare to network?

A. Read several current event articles of possible interest and be ready to share. Place your contact information in your right outer jacket pocket, if no jacket put them in your right trouser pocket. The right is referenced because the left is where you would put the cards that you receive. Have in mind what professional contacts and information you would like to leave with.

If you don't have a pocket you should maintain easy access to your contact information. Remember to keep your right hand available for that unexpected handshake.

Q. I just took a bite, and someone asks me a question, what should I do?

A: Nod, then finish chewing and answer the question. It is also an excellent idea to practice taking small bites referred to as the "ten chew;" after ten chews you swallow.

Q. Should you shake hands once the food is served?

A: If at all possible avoid shaking hands once the food is served. Always keep cultural differences in mind. If it's a high ranking official with your organization or someone you would like to develop a relationship, offer a brief hand shake. Should you feel the need to wipe your hand afterward do so on the unused part of the napkin, preferably without drawing attention.

Q. When there isn't a host/hostess for the event and food is served, what should you do first serve yourself or meet other people?

A. You may join the beverage or food areas, both are ideal gathering points. Introduce yourself, then serve your plate. However, never give the appearance that the food is the reason for attending.

Q. When food is served and a blessing is not a part of the program, what should I do?

A. When everyone is served at your table, say a brief grace silently. When you bow your head most likely, the others will be quiet for a moment. Be brief to show respect for their time and understanding; then proceed with the meal.

Application of the above situations mixed with common sense; will empower you to enjoy seamless encounters during your entire career. – Helen Rogers

Testimony of a successful professional in their own words:

"I was at a Christmas gathering at my company. They had a variety of cookies. A section head wearing a black suit selected cookies covered with white powdered sugar. It was a hard cookie and at every bite the cookie exploded covering his black suit with the white powder...he tried to brush it off, BUT it just seemed to spread over the fabric."

"When I went to events it was not to eat or to drink alcohol... I was very careful to select cookies or food that would be easy to eat and NOT messy. If you select the fried chicken and eat it as it can best be eaten using your hands; then if you meet someone who wants to shake your hand you extend a greasy hand...not good! If they had hot dogs NO mustard for me just the hot dog...mustard has a habit of getting on your tie."

"I also ate little and I ate fast, then I was able to present my points to the others while they were eating. I was not there to eat, I was there to connect...I would eat lightly before I arrived or after I returned home. Some gorged on the free food, had sauces on their hands, face and suits...and some were half drunk...not a good look before influential others."

GIFTS FOR VARIOUS OCCASIONS

Hostess Gifts

Floral arrangement sent the day before the event, assorted teas, elegant note paper, fringed cocktail napkin, souvenir of interest from one of your recent trips, nuts, jams, taper candles, vintage books, rich chocolates, a personalized bottle of wine, a small elegant frame for the photographer, Tidbit bowls with a wood tray, painted leather coasters, Nutshell's nut bars, Amazon Echo or Goat's milk glycerin soap are good examples.

Cultures or Special Days

When selecting a gift one should consider the position within the organization of the recipient, the nature of the celebration, and the culture of the receiver.

In Japan a knife set or items with a sharp edge or point; signify a severing of the relationship.

In India avoid gifts made of leather. The cow is considered sacred.

Hanukkah — Fruit baskets, chocolates, holiday doormat, shortbread, glasses, candles, charms, Gourmet chocolate berries, candle finger puppets, and assorted coffee are excellent choices available in various shapes, colors, and sizes.

Kwanzaa — Fruit baskets, seven candles set, pave heart, circle charm, seven principles of Kwanzaa plaque, socks, decorative pillow, pajamas, mugs, twilight lanterns, table mats, custom chocolate bars, and assorted gourmet items.

Gifts for Supervisors and Co-workers

Cookies and candies – use expressive baskets, trays or boxes.

Conversation trays – Crystal or silver.

Flowers – fresh cut, potted or waterless. The height should be moderate making it adaptable to most homes or office furnishings.

Gift Baskets – with unique shapes and weaves filled with various edible and non-edible items in different wrappings expresses an air of excitement as the recipient opens them.

Gourmet coffee, teas, cheeses, unique processed meat products, ham, and sausage are high on the list of favorites.

Sports items – Gift certificates or cards (verify the expiration and exchange policy), magazine subscription, tickets to area events or souvenirs from a unique global location.

Volunteer Exposure Gift – Invite the person to join you at a soup kitchen, food pantry, homeless shelter or the local community center; sharing of ourselves with others is very rewarding; for the person with everything.

Charity or Community Service Organizations – welcomes monetary or workforce gifts.

Collectibles — Why not contribute to their existing collection of equal or higher value guaranteeing your donation a special place on the display shelf.

Personally made Items – including perishable and non-perishable food items sends a message from the heart.

Gag Bag Gift Giving – Think about how you would feel if you received the gag gift you are about to wrap. Then think of the audience. If you still feel comfortable — go for it. The selection may range from vintage clothing items to Granny slippers and all stops in between. When making your choice remember you will still be working with those individuals after the laughter is over.

TIPPING — HOME AND ABROAD

How to Pay

Cash or credit: Either is fine. If you're paying with a credit card, it's okay to leave the tip on the card. The server will receive it in a day or so directly in their account.

Amount or Percentages to give in America

The following are strongly recommended to show our appreciation for the services we are receiving. However, the quality of service may also be reflected in the tip.

- Sit-down restaurants: 20 percent — always. In the last few years, the precise amount you tip is widely understood to be around 20 percent.
- Food trucks: Add a buck or two.
- Bars: One dollar per drink at dives, 20 percent at cocktail bars.
- Bakeries and Coffee shops: One dollar or more is acceptable, depending on the type of service requested.
- Fast-Casual Counter service: 20 percent is expected.
- Delivery: Five dollar minimum is expected, more depending on the number of items delivered.

When making your list of how much you plan to pay for each gift, keep in mind what the receiver would like and not just what you want to give. Think about what you know about the person. Do they have a specific eating place, or attend certain sports events. If the answer is yes, then why not give them a gift card to one of those places.

When there are budget constraints, consider giving a "thank you" gift during the year and a smaller gift at the end of the year.

Your Home Helpers

- Housekeepers: The tip should be the cost of one cleaning. If there is a team, consider tipping the teammates individually, and privately.

- Trash Collectors: Check the local guidelines for tipping "public-service workers" first. If there are no restrictions, give ten to twenty-five dollars per person. This may be monetary gifts or gift cards.

- Lawn Maintenance/Landscaper: Considering that they are seasonal their hours will vary in peak months, so more is being considerate of their responsibilities give twenty to fifty dollars.

- Pool Service: One should give the equivalent of one week's service.

- Apartment Superintendent: Twenty to eighty dollars, you may think that this sounds high, did you consider that they are on call 24/7. You can give more if you think he or she has done a "superb" job.

- Doorman: Whatever you give, consider giving each doorman the same amount to be fair. Twenty to one hundred dollars is average. However, you also should keep in mind their total areas of service.

- Parking or Garage Attendants: Ten to fifty dollars are the norm.

- Handymen, Exterminators, and other Home-Service Providers: Twenty to one hundred dollars is a given, more if extenuating circumstances were involved.

Loved One's Caregivers

- Day Care Teacher: Twenty to seventy dollars, plus a small gift from your child is the average.

- School Teachers: Consider a small gift or gift card. Don't forget a gift for the teacher's aide or paraprofessional.

- Principal, School Nurse, and School Secretary: A small gift or card will get the job done.

- Bus Driver, Lunch Aide: Twenty – five dollars is the standard gift, and represents all the children.

- Babysitter: An evening's pay, plus a small gift from your child is workable.

- Nanny: One week's to one month's pay, plus a small gift from your child. When thinking about the amount, keep in mind their total responsibility.

- Pet Sitter/Dog Walker: A cash gift equivalent to one service.

- Pet Groomer: The gift should be equivalent to one visit.

Package Deliveries

- U.S. Mail Carrier: Federal regulations guidelines indicates that you can only give a gift worth twenty dollars or less. If you are watching your budget, consider giving to the Carrier that delivers regularly.

- UPS/FedEx Delivery Person: UPS drivers, give a small gift or twenty to twenty-five dollars. While UPS prefers drivers to receive gifts, it is at the customer's discretion. FedEx drivers are allowed to accept tips and gifts up to seventy-four dollars.

- Newspaper Delivery Person: A gift of ten to thirty dollars is standard.

Tipping for Other Services

Here are recommended tipping amounts for a range of other service people you may do business with.

- Car wash attendant: At pickup give three to five bucks.

- Tattoo artist: Ten to twenty percent is expected.

- Tow truck driver: A tip is expected between three and five dollars, even if your car insurance or AAA is footing the bill. Would you say it was terrific for the person to assist you in your time of stress? Yes, it's their job; however, a tip will help their attitude about their situation.

- Shoe shiner: Two to three bucks are typical.

- Furniture delivery people: A five to ten dollar tip per worker is normal, depending on how heavy the item is.

- Movers: If a cross country moving company team is hauling your furniture, many experts suggest tipping five percent of your total bill, but this isn't etched in stone. Tip-insensitive consumers wouldn't think about tipping moving company employees. Therefore, most movers would be happy to get some "cold water or a soft drink" for their services.

Tipping on the Road

- Airport or train porter: One to two dollars are standard, more for extra services.

- Cab driver: Depending on how long you had to wait, the speed of the cab, your comfort level and how safe you feel during the drive; ten to eighteen percent is average.

- Hotel concierge: The tip is usually given at your departure for ten to twenty dollars.

- Hotel maid: The tip should be offered each day in the amount of two to three bucks. Please leave it with a note of thanks and the maid will know it is for them.

- Delivery: Apps like UberEats and Postmates don't require tips, yet, some offer suggested gratuities on their checkout page. GrubHub founder strongly encourages a ten to fifteen percent tip. After all, delivery drivers aren't salaried workers, and they're delivering food straight to your door in all types of conditions.

- Takeout: You're not required to tip for takeout, according to some etiquette experts. A gratuity is recommended for extra services like curbside delivery or unusually large complicated orders, in the amount of ten percent.

- Buffet: Rules for wait staff at a buffet is similar to that of delivery. A pre-tax amount of ten percent is considered standard by most protocol research.

- Bar Tip Jar: Tip jars are fairly universal at bars, cafés, and coffee shops, and this can cause some confusion about tipping. However, customers are not obligated to tip unless they received exceptional service.

- Bad service: If the service is inferior, leave a ten percent tip. Your amount will reflect the service and management will be made aware. This will be noticeable in restaurants where the tips are divided among the team so not tipping could affect more than just your server.

Five Tipping Myths

Haven't we all wondered about when to tip, whom to tip and how much? Let's expose five myths to help guide you on your next outing.

1. There is no need to tip a hotel housekeeper

The average hourly pay for U.S. hotel housekeepers is $9.21 according to the UNITE HERE union. Let's consider their job. On a typical day, a staffer may be responsible for fifteen or more rooms. They have to scrub fifteen bathrooms, changed fifteen sets of sheets, and vacuumed fifteen rooms in seven or eight hours? Hotels with resent bed upgrades, they have to lift those heavy pillow-top mattresses.

My Story: *"I once worked as a housekeeper, and survived one day. Pulling, lifting and bending was more than I could handle physically as a twenty-year-old in good health."*

2. A restaurant server's tip will receive the same amount whether you use cash or a credit card.

Don't be so sure. Some eateries require the waiters and bartenders to pay the credit-card company service fee on the gratuity of two to three percent. Servers most likely will not get credit-card tips the day of the service, which means employers will have time to fudge on the amount given.

3. The hotel concierge should be rewarded for every reservation or arrangement she or he makes.

Yes, the concierges do rely on tips to boost their incomes. However, they don't necessarily expect one for giving simple directions or a quick phone call for an easy event reservation. You should consider giving a tip after the event is over, in case it didn't meet your expectations.

There are times when the concierge receives a kickback when they recommend certain attractions. If you tip when making the appointment and the place isn't to your liking you have limited recourse. If you are asking for something out of the ordinary, you should give more than the standard ten percent tip.

4. Those room-service fees go *straight* to the staffer.

Don't count on it. Bills are hard to decode, and hotel policies vary. A service charge is usually a tip, but it might be pooled among the room-service team, and in some cases, the hotel, and can be less than 20%. If you want to reward excellent service, ask the server what percentage he or she is getting and give them that amount.

5. I have to *accept* the automatic daily gratuity added to my bill by the cruise line.

No, you don't have to accept the amount. Cruisers use to routinely hand over envelopes containing tokens of appreciation for stewards, waiters, and others at the end of cruising. But today, most of the major cruise lines add extra dollars per day to ensure that low-paid employees get a tip.

If you disagree with the additional charges, go to the purser's office and ask that totals be adjusted downward — or up. However, before you go, think about what services the tips are covering? Remember that, right or wrong, those doing the unskilled jobs on the ship rely on tips as the mainstay of their pay.

Mental Tip Calculations

Try one of these two useful tricks to calculate tips:

- If you are tipping 15 percent, multiply the pre-tax amount by 10 percent and then add half of that amount.

- A 20 percent tip is simple to calculate. Just figure out 10 percent of the bill and multiply by two.

Whether you're using an upscale restaurant or the local pizza place, as the recipient of a delicious meal; you should make sure the delivery person is tipped appropriately. This is their source of income, and they made sure that you could enjoy it in the privacy of your home or office.

If you have special requests or requirements, such as a large party, young children who have made a mess, or special dietary restrictions, it's considerate and fair to leave a slightly higher tip.

TIPPING ABROAD
NOT REQUIRED BUT ACCEPTED

Tipping usually isn't mandatory; however, it is customary for most cultures. How do you know if you're in a country where tipping is a prerequisite or virtually unheard of? Tipping etiquette varies by region and can lead to embarrassing situations at business dinners if you're not in the know. Rounding up the check may be acceptable in one area, but an insult in others.

Consider the following guidelines when traveling abroad, and avoid the judgmental eye of clients during your next dining experience.

As you begin globe-trotting, one of the most valuable pieces of information anyone can offer is awareness of the unspoken rules of tipping etiquette in your country of destination.

Knowing when, who, and how to tip is almost essential for any traveler; it will show your knowledge and respect of the culture. Sometimes you will receive better services and, unexpected favors will come your way.

Tipping is almost a world-wide practice, however, as you travel to different countries, it quickly becomes apparent that it isn't practiced in the same way in every culture.

Australia

Neither Australia nor New Zealand adds service charges to bills, tipping is not a common practice.

Continental Europe and the Mediterranean

In this region, tipping is not required, although it is normal and acceptable to leave a percentage of the bill.

In St. Barthes, there are no service charges, but the unwritten rule is to tip 15 percent.

Countries such as China, South Korea, and Japan, are all no-tip cultures leaving a gratuity for someone is not only virtually unheard of but can cause confusion. Some places consider it as rude.

TIPPING IS REQUIRED AND APPRECIATED

In Morocco, if the tip isn't included in the bill, a 10 percent tip is expected. The standard in South Africa is 15 percent. Your tip should always be in the currency of the country you're in.

In Egypt, most restaurants include a tip in the bill, and the customers are expected to give an additional 5 -10 percent.

In Tanzania, your tip could be the exchange of items such as watches, brand-name clothing or other things of value. Cash is welcomed, offering to help pay for school fees is more readily acceptable.

In most Southeast Asian countries, at least a 10 percent tip is expected.

In Europe, there is one general rule across the board: Tip in cash, not a credit card. The standard tip for a waiter is about 10 percent, only moving to 15 percent if the service is exceptional.

Latin America

Tipping is not a big part of the culture in some areas, but 8 to 12 percent is appreciated.

In Brazil, your bill will include the tip, and extra is required.

In Chile's upscale restaurants, 10 percent is added to the bill. An additional 5-7percent tip is expected.

In Canada, the minimum tip is 15 percent, with an additional service charge.

In Mexico, the rule of thumb is 10 to 15 percent is added to your bill, and your additional tip should be in pesos. That is their way of saying we are our own country, not an extension of the US.

South Pacific

In Dominica, the service charge is typically added to the bill, and the customer is expected to tip 10 percent.

South America

In Bolivia, a tip might be given in addition to the service charge included in the bill.

In Argentina, a more common practice is for customers to add a 10 percent tip, and also round up the bill.

Northern Europe

In the United Kingdom, the rule of 10 to 15 percent tip is quite familiar. Some establishments will add a percentage to the bill.

In Norway and Denmark, a tip is included in the bill.

In Sweden and Finland, a gratuity is often included. If the bill doesn't have a gratuity already factored in, the locals will tip by rounding up or leaving small change.

In Germany, a tip is added to the bill, if not, some small change should be left.

In the Middle East, most countries will add a percentage to the bill, they expect an additional tip also. You are supposed to tip for just about anything, such as holding a door open or pointing out something in a museum (even if you can see it for yourself!) The culture is very forward about asking for a tip, which generally makes up a large portion of a worker's salary. You don't automatically have to give a tip, just because someone asked for one.

In India, but not in Dubai, a 10 percent service charge is automatically added to bills.

BEAUTY TIPPING IN AMERICA

Consider these pointers on your next beauty visit. How often have you stood at the counter waiting for your credit card thinking do I have enough cash for the tip? Make tipping easy for yourself, the same rule applies as in other venues. The minimum is 15 to 20 percent when you received special treatment. Remember extra tips will help to ensure that you will be treated with kindness.

Have you ever questioned if you should tip for a pedicure and manicure when done by the same person?

The Nail Salon

A regular manicure is 15 percent, gel, acrylics and exceptional treatment 20 percent. When getting a manicure and pedicure you should tip as if two technicians were involved — two areas of the body was pampered, and a 20 percent tip for each treatment is reasonable.

The Hair Salon

Have you ever said I am only getting a trim, why 20 percent? The percentage is the same regardless of the service required for regular customers. However, if you are a first-timer, you can get away with giving 15 percent. Once you get to know your stylist between 20 and 25 percent is the rule. Remember to provide an extra tip or nice gift during the holidays.

The Blow Dry Bar

The stylist should be tipped 20 percent at the blow dry bar. To receive the services we have become to enjoy, give a proper tip to ensure it every visit.

The Bikini Wax Salon

Did you say bikini waxing? One slip and oh well! You should always be generous when tipping, giving 20 to 25 percent minimum.

The Brow/Lash Bar

15 percent is okay when getting a quick clean-up around your brows. However, if you're getting them shaped or tinted, you should tip 20 percent. Tip 20 to 25 percent for eyelash extensions or lash perms. Those services require attention to detail and time for the perfect you.

The Spa

You should tip your spa expert 20 to 25 percent for facials, peels or massages. When you receive even better treatment than usual, go ahead and tip more. To be generous is always a great idea!

Personal Trainer

Your tip should be the cost of one session, if your visit is complementary give a small gift.

Masseuse

You may give a small gift or up to the cost of one session.

Giving a tip or gift is considered a unique way of telling the person that rendered the service that you truly appreciate how they enhanced your lifestyle.

Protocol for the HealthCare Community

HOSPITAL PROTOCOL

Wow! You want to visit a friend in the hospital, but realize that you haven't visited in a long time. Now fear of the unknown is setting in. Relax, there's a code of conduct to help you understand the world of healthcare on each facility's website. One thing you should be aware of is the privacy policy changes. Only the patient's healthcare power of attorney will be provided with sensitive updates, regardless of your relationship to the patient. Consider these suggestions before visiting.

Can You Visit Anytime?

It depends on your relationship or legal responsibility for the patient. The normal visiting hours are listed on the hospital's website. One question is, does the patient feel up to having visitors? Most patients value their privacy and need rest. They also may not like visitors while they are hooked up to machines or other equipment. If the patient is seriously ill or heavy medicated, he or she generally is not up to talking.

Your relationship with the patient may not be in question, but he or she must be mentally and physically in a receiving mode. Should you arrive and the patient doesn't appear to be alert and receptive, check with the nurse or a family member and possibly consider returning in a few days. You may wish to call to check on the patient's progress in the interim.

Hospital Visiting Hours Serves a Purpose

This is an undeniable fact; unlimited visiting hours can be exhausting and may delay the recovery of the patient. It is imperative that the patient has adequate uninterrupted periods of rest to heal. When it's time for the patient to receive personal care and you are asked to leave the room, then excuse yourself and leave promptly. Never over-stay your visit. Hospitals are not social venues.

Message of A Closed Door

Please knock and wait for permission to enter. How long do you have to wait? Wait until the door is opened and you are permitted to enter. After a few minutes with no response, visit the nurse's station. You can't guess what is taking place in the room. The patient may be getting some much needed rest or perhaps even a bath. Don't assume anything, and do not enter without permission.

How Long to Visit?

The length of time depends on the patient and your observation of his or her condition. In a critical situation, there may be a limit of visiting time posted. After all, this isn't the time to catch your friend up on all they have missed. Some patients tire easily but may be too polite to ask you to leave. Remember that you're not likely to be the only visitor and having many visitors can be exhausting and slow the healing process.

Asking About Surgical or Test Results

Medical information is considered private. If the patient doesn't share it with you, please don't ask or comment about the readings on the machines.

Appropriate Gift Ideas

Consider checking with the patient's nurse or family before you make your purchase. Most facilities will have a gift shop nearby if you wait until your arrival to get the gift. Flowers, cards, and balloons sometimes take space needed for the patient's care and are a nuisance when the patient is discharged. A gift card to the patient's favorite store has become very popular and also gives the patient a day trip to look forward to in the future. After surgery, a patient usually can't eat certain foods, so candy and other food items may not be a good idea. If in doubt, ask about dietary restrictions; don't just bring what you wish.

How about a simple get well or thinking of you card or a tiny stuffed animal? Think about the patient's hobby and bring something that will make them feel like getting back in the shop or outdoors. Books of crossword puzzles, magazines, or word-search will give them something to help pass the time. One can only watch so much television media coverage or play games.

Share Encouraging News

When visiting a co-worker, talking about budget cuts or layoffs aren't comforting. If you are aware of a disturbing story from the workplace, ask yourself, "Am I the right person to bring this news?" While what you know may be true, the question is, are you the person to pass it on? Disturbing news doesn't help the healing process. Think about a time when a situation made you feel ill, and you weren't in the hospital.

Well, it is worse when someone is post-surgery or under medication. Please allow your friend to recover to the point where they can handle unpleasant news. Gossip is always inappropriate.

Time seems to drag by when you are in the hospital. Reassure your friend that their co-workers, church family, and neighbors are concerned about them and are looking forward to their return. Encouraging news will help keep the person connected to their world of comfort. The feeling of isolation can cause a delay in the recovery time brought on by depression.

If the medical condition is extremely delicate or critical, you may not know what to say. The best approach is to observe the individual's expressions, and then choose your words carefully. Sometimes a smile or comforting touch is best. If the patient wants to talk, be a considerate listener. Never point out that the patient looks ill; they know that. After all, that is why they are in the hospital. Try to remain uplifting and encourage the patient to have a healthy, positive attitude.

Don't sit on the bed when trying to comfort. Also be mindful of touching the person, sometimes their body is more sensitive than it appears. If the patient is feeling sad or hopeless, try to lift their spirits with kindness. Wear a smile. Share funny memories and try to get them to think about the fun times you'll have in the future once they are feeling better.

Untiring Support is a Challenge

A hospitalized person is dealing with physically, mentally and emotional discomfort. They may need someone to run errands or to check the house and/or business affairs as well as emotional support during this challenging time. Stress will cause the patient's emotions to be off the chart, from hopeful to fearful to angry or to even denial. Never tell the individual how he or she should feel. Accept the way they are reacting without criticizing or questioning them.

Gently ask if they want to talk or if there is something you can do to help them or their family. Never share your sorrow or fear with the patient. You are there to encourage. Never expect the patient to entertain you as guess in their home. They are not home, and isn't feeling the best in most cases. When you schedule your visit make sure you have time to talk, and share some type of entertainment that the patient will enjoy.

In many cases the patient may not be able to care for themselves after a stay in the hospital. This is where additional care will become necessary, and caregivers will be added to the healthcare team. Let's look at some of the responsibilities of the caregiver.

MY THOUGHTS

_____

_____

_____

_____

_____

_____

_____

_____

_____

_____

_____

_____

_____

_____

_____

_____

_____

_____

_____

THE CAREGIVER

When you are the Caregiver

If the patient has a chronic condition and will be going through a lengthy recovery, your on-going support is essential. Many people will be there the first week, but your friend or relative will need help throughout the recovery period.

Now that you are the patient's caregiver, you may find yourself physically and emotionally exhausted after a while. It is imperative to have a plan of action before agreeing to help.

Nine Areas to Consider

Know who is in charge of the patient's affairs and their contact information.

- Verify the schedule for each shift, and where the contact information is located.

- Who will cover an emergency?

- What to do in case of a no-show?

- Confirm whether you expect to be paid and, if so, the amount.

- If appropriate, notify the person in charge that you are volunteering and advise for how long.

- What information you are allowed to share and with whom?

- What are your overall duties?

- Are there limits or restrictions regarding visitors?

Once the schedule is worked out, advise the patient who will be with them at what times. This should help the patient relax, knowing when a staff person versus a visitor is entering the room.

If you are on duty and start feeling overwhelmed, take a short break if the person doesn't need constant visual care. Sometimes a breath of fresh air will revive you.

My Story

Doing my fifth year as a caregiver, I needed an extended break. My need for sleep had increased, and my appetite and health changed. There were some changes in my own job performance which could have affected the safety of others.

I was experiencing four of the nine signs of depression. Depression didn't cross my mind, I just thought I was overly tired. I visited my doctor, and he said I had an abnormal stress level and would need to change my schedule immediately; medication would not help.

As the saying goes, "the receiver-of-care will out-live the caregiver, unless the caregiver keeps their own health in mind." To prevent caregiver burn-out, one must know their own limitations.

To serve others is considered a blessing, and can be rewarding under the proper conditions.

Ten Warning Signs of Caregiver Fatigue

- Lack of energy.

- Sleep problems, too much or too little.

- Changes in eating habits, weight loss or gain.

- A feeling of hopelessness.

- Withdrawing from, or losing interest in, activities you once enjoyed.

- Neglecting your own physical and emotional needs.

- Feeling like caregiving is controlling your life.

- Becoming unusually impatient with the person you're caring for and/or others.

- Depression or mood swings.

- Headaches, stomachaches, and other physical problems.

Fatigue Prevention

Now that you know what to look for, here are some pointers to help you avoid a breakdown.

Ask for Help

Needing help doesn't make you a bad person. It means you can't do it alone.

Breaks are Okay

Visit with friends. Take a long bath. Listen to your favorite music.

Take Care of Yourself First

Never skip your own doctor's appointments because of others. Do exercises and eat well, and don't sacrifice sleep.

Put "Me time" on your Schedule

Enjoy your favorite hot beverage. Journal about your struggles. Meditate, pray, and exercise.

Make a List of Your Daily Activities

See if you can delegate something. Maybe a family member can make dinner, and/or carry-in or dine-out on different days, instead of cooking. Perhaps a friend or relative can help with household tasks. When people offer to help — take them up on it! Review the Family-leave Policy at work.

If your loved one is receiving hospice care, ask your contact about referrals for local emotional support groups. Communicating with others may help relieve your frustrations. Share your struggles and joys with others who understand.

Schedule a brief get-a-way for yourself, with the help of hospice respite care. They offer short-term inpatient admission up to five days and nights maximum. The time away is for family members or others caring for a patient at home.

There is support, there are shortcuts, and there is the reorganization of priorities which may enable you to be a happier person, enjoying what has been assigned.

Helping others with their families' health issues can challenge our time, knowledge, and relationship with the patient.

Would you say health issues are high on a family's list of concerns these days? As human beings we desire to help others, however, quite often we do not count-up the total cost of the responsibility.

Helping Friends with Health Issues in the Home

Let's review some pertinent areas of interest before you agree to help your friend.

- When scheduling a visit, try to clear your day since you don't know what you will be asked to do. If you can only stay a certain length of time, ask the person what you can do to help within your limited time-frame.

- Privacy must be respected regardless of the person's age. When you enter their room, and it's evident that the person is improperly dressed, stop and avert your eyes in order to give the person a chance to adjust. In the case of a relative, and you have access to the home, call their name as you enter the house to avoid startling the person. Regardless of the severity of one's illness, their dignity must be respected.

- Focus on the most obvious need of the person you are visiting, keeping in mind that you can't be everything to every person. Don't make promises you can't fulfill. Be observant of the person's expressions, their body language or their tone, as these may be the key indicators of how they are feeling or what they are thinking. Try to match your demeanor with theirs, unless it is obvious their spirit needs a lift.

- Pay attention to what is being said and how it is being conveyed. It's often difficult for some people to express how they are feeling. The visitor's personal problems or opinion should not be part of the conversation with the person they are visiting.

- Strike the right attitude by your actions or reactions. Never give the impression that you are not concerned, by folding your arms, avoiding eye contact, or providing a short answer to repeated questions.

- Don't be quick to judge. Its human nature to make a quick judgment call about a given situation. However, your judgment must not come across in a condescending tone of voice or answer.

- Open-ended questions will encourage the person to describe what and how they are feeling. Listen, and you may get some unexpected information. If you ask, are you in pain or uncomfortable? The answer will be "yes or no," which leads to follow-up questions that may produce the wrong emotion. Always reflect an attitude of sincere concern, and not one of "I was only trying to help you."

- Offering reassurance should make the person feel comfortable. Always give them the best answers possible without violating their privacy. Even if you have experienced the same situation, be careful about using the phrase "I know how you feel." All cases are different.

- Choosing your words with care can help avoid possible negative expressions. Don't say, "There's nothing wrong, or there's not a problem." Consider saying, "everything will be fine." When sharing information about a severe issue consider saying, "it's essential to follow up on this." The words "serious, dangerous or emergency" send a warning that something is alarming. Your relationship with the patient will help determine the expressions you choose.

- You must control your time. For example, if you get a call from a shut-in friend that they need you to come by today, you might agree to pop by when you really don't have the time. When you hear their repeated concern, don't be upset or rude. Simply repeat what you think is the request, and ask how you can help. Your friend's reply could be a shocker: "I'm not looking for help;" "I just want to talk about it."

STOP! Watch your tone and body language. After all this is your friend. Merely say, "Now I understand," and explain about your time constraints. Don't promise to come back at a particular time, unless you can fulfill that commitment.

My Experience: I have a senior friend who would call me and say, "Can you come by after work in the morning?" "We need to talk about some things." After several visits, I learned to ask questions so I would have the right mindset upon my arrival. Sometimes he would say. "My wife isn't feeling well and wanted to see you." Sometimes he just wanted a listening ear. When the call is related to the family, I prayed for the energy to do whatever was necessary to help. After all, I realized that my parents, who lived out of state, made some of the same types of calls, and I was grateful for the help they received from others close by.

During some of my visits, when I found myself no longer actively listening, I would say, "Is there anything else we need to go over today?" He would usually say, "No, that's about it." We promised to keep in touch, and I would leave.

*We must control our time in love,
even if we can't fulfill the request immediately.*

CHOOSING A SUITABLE RETIREMENT FACILITY

It's time for a family member to make that all-significant change in their life called downsizing their home. The new location may be in a retirement community, assisted living, or full-time care unit. Diligent homework must begin with the entire family in mind.

During the process of reducing the household items, allow the loved one to have a reasonable input as to what they would like to keep for their new home. If it won't fit, calmly explain the situation with the family member and move on. Do not argue, as that will only make things worse. Focus attention on the positive aspects of the new arrangements.

The adjustment period is very challenging for the person who is making the move, so do your best to make the move as seamless as possible.

Discuss the Move in Advance

Schedule a time to discuss the need for your loved one to move from their current resident, preferably in advance. Allow the loved one time to digest the results of the situation. Have some brochures ready or use a website, depending on the setting. Listen to their reasons for not wanting to change, then explain why the family feels that it is in everyone's best interest to consider the move.

If the conversation isn't progressing in the right direction, change the subject to something more positive. Always emphasize the family's love and gratefulness for the individual, as well as the positive side of making the change. Ask him or her how they are feeling and then listen to gain your best understanding.

Consider talking to the member's medical team for assistance in encouraging the loved one that the move is not only appropriate, but advisable for them. If the member is experiencing health issues and isn't in the mindset to help with the decision, choose a facility that will best meet the loved one's needs. Ask for references and personally meet the staff members.

Take a tour of the place you are considering for the family member. Let your loved one visit the rooms, activity, and dining areas. Talk to the staff about the in-house programs and off-site events. The external grounds and landscape should be considered in the tour, especially if your loved one is used to having gardens or living in a country setting. Also, ask to see a roster of residents to determine whether any friends or acquaintances may already be residing there.

Planning the Move

If the loved one is capable, allow them to choose the community. This will give a sense of ownership and independence when making such a significant change in their life. If possible, schedule the move over a few days. Give the family member time to reflect on the memories of the items that will not be going to the new place.

The move will be an emotional time for the entire family especially if a "long-term home place" is involved. Take some photos, and reflect on how you would feel if you were moving.

Reminisce on memories of times past. Try and correlate your feelings to your loved one's concerns. Be sensitive to the person's moods, while consistently moving forward with the schedule.

Settling In

Stay actively involved in your family member's life with unscheduled visits and calls, especially over the first few months. This will help to avoid loneliness, isolation or depression, which can happen without notice. Help the loved one adjust to their new lifestyle by asking about their activities, and the names of their neighbors. If they can't give you one name or can't remember any of the events, this could be a cause for concern.

Discuss the transition progress with staff members. They see the situation from a daily perspective.

If loneliness or depression is suspected, ask for input from the staff. Sometimes the person wants to make you feel guilty for them being there, even though they had a say in the move. When this is the case, consider sharing a meal with them, or watching a movie. Spending time there during one of the activities will give you a better understanding of the situation. Don't dismiss or minimize the time it takes to adjust to the new living environment. Expecting happiness overnight isn't being realistic.

Getting Involved

Retirement communities offer a wide selection of events including arts, exercise classes, field trips, lectures, games, sporting events, and more. It's important for the resident to get involved with something of interest and not simply wait for their family to visit. Making new friends will increase the feeling of community and security.

Addressing Concerns

If something doesn't feel right or your loved one appears agitated, sad, confused or angry most of the time, talk to the staff. Discuss their health issues and social life. Quite often, the lack of necessary social changes will hinder progress in the new environment.

Signs of continued depression, memory loss, or aggressive or other abnormal behavior should be discussed with their medical advisor.

NURSING HOME VISITS DURING THE HOLIDAYS AND OTHER SEASONS

Have you ever visited a nursing home at Christmas? If so, did you notice how many others pick that time also? Christmas is the most common family-and-friend connection time of the year. There is a spirit of giving in the air, and the residents of nursing homes are high on the list of receivers. Well, who are some of those visitors, and why? The menu consists of infrequent visitors, community groups, families bringing their grandchildren, and church-sponsored activities, to name a few.

When you see the expressions of hope on the faces of the residences, taking time to visit can be rewarding. If you are a casual or first-time visitor, these are some simple tips to remember.

Schedule Your Visit

Your call will not only ensure that you won't interrupt previously planned visitors, meal, rest, or social activities; it enables residents to be prepared and excited about your visit.

Do Your Homework

Some residents may have physical disabilities or difficulty with hearing, vision, or movement. Other residents may have memory issues or issues participating in conversations. Before you visit, ask a staff member for an update or visit the facility's website covering the topic.

Knock Before Entering the Room

The residents' rooms are their homes and represent their private space. It is polite to ask permission before entering a room or touching their personal items. The residents will likely welcome questions about photos, decorations, or other items; this is an excellent conversation starter.

Be a Good Listener

Elderly residents are wonderful historians and usually love to share. Providing a friendly and attentive ear will be gratifying not only to your elderly friend or relative, but will likely be a captivating experience for you as well.

Residents and Volunteer Energy Level

Nursing home residents often become tired quickly, and 20-30 minutes may be an exhausting visit for them. On the other hand, if you both are enjoying a conversation or game, don't rush to finish if all is going well.

It is not advisable to plan a visit when you are tired, limited on time, or expect to see more than one resident. There is no way to determine the mood or energy level of the resident you will visit, therefore you may need to give more of yourself than expected.

Prepare to Share

Bring an inspirational book, photo, or card with you. Some residents will talk freely, while others may sit and stare. You will need to be creative and dispel the silences. You may consider offering to write or read for residents who may have trouble with these activities. If the person appears tired or dozes during your visit, quietly excuse yourself and leave.

Return Visits

Don't promise to visit again unless you truly intend to follow through, you may also put it on your calendar right then. Many nursing home residents get very few visitors, and breaking an appointment is depressing for your friend or relative. If you can't keep the date, call in advance and let the staff know, so they can plan an activity.

Know Your Comfort Zone

Some volunteers relate better to patients with certain limitations, be sure to make the activity coordinator aware of your desire when scheduling the visit.

Visiting Various Ages

Everyone's length of life will vary, some will die young while others will live much longer. The length of life within my family varied from age sixteen to age eighty-four. The sixteen-year-old had one season, ten years plus six. The eighty-four-year-old had four ten's plus four years. Learning to share with someone in various seasons requires patience as well as specific personal skills to develop the desired memories.

My winter season experiences are a direct result of being asked to volunteer to help family and friends as a teenager. Before choosing to say yes, it is important to check, not only our availability but also your ability to handle stressful situations with grace. Accepting rejections beyond your control will come up.

During our fall season, life's status often changes from couples to singles. Desiring someone for companionship while maintaining our ability to carry out the activities of daily living with ease is normal. It is the winter season that will often require full-time help to address the significant changes in the physical and mental lives of the individual and their families. At this point, the visitor must monitor their emotional levels, if they are to serve and maintain their own good health.

Winter Season What-ifs

In a healthcare facility, you might walk into the room of a friend and the roommate is enjoying the program on the television to the extent that they are screaming at the characters, but you intended to read one of your friend's favorite poems. No, you can't ask the person to leave the room. It's their home also, and rescheduling your visit isn't an option. So what is the solution?

Consider asking the roommate if they would like to hear one of the poems from your book. If they say "yes," your situation is resolved. If they say "no," ask permission to change the volume, or you may want to consider taking your friend to another area of the facility. Expressing a negative frustrated attitude will not get the job done; since most people in their winter seasons aren't attentive to your conversation or body language.

When taking flowers or other decorative items to a nursing home, consider contacting the staff in advance, as this can be very helpful concerning space availability in the residents rooms or the common areas. Keep in mind that your gift is welcomed in most instances; however, large plants can limit the space required for activities. Some groups will bring instruments, and a podium may be necessary.

Inspirational Winter Season Sharing

This service requires careful planning, including a pre-visit to the facility. The age group is not always responsive to what is going on around them; therefore, the program should consist of action songs that encourage participation. The songs should be in large print, making it easier for the residents to sing along. Speaking from my experience as a presenter, sharing this kind of hospitality requires diligence, but is very rewarding.

Areas to Consider

- Keep in the front of your mind that your tone is the key to reach the attendees. As they enter the room, speak to each one sharing a smile, and a positive comment – a supportive way of increasing their comfort level.

- Encourage them to participate by asking about their favorite songs or scripture verses. Be mindful to remember names or something said during the previous visit, which is crucial to the "winter generation."

- Remember, the schedule is of the utmost importance and should be adhered to within reason. The staff is responsible for keeping the residents on schedule, and it is your responsibility to help them to achieve their goals.

My Experience: During one of my visits, the State was conducting an audit of the facility. If someone were off schedule, it would affect their rating, which could have reflected negatively of my abilities to follow instructions; and our local assembly as a positive contributor to the community. Inspections are random; my experience was on a Sunday.

Cancellations of Availability

The contact person should be notified of cancellations as soon as possible, thus allowing time to make changes to the activities for the day. In our *winter season,* disappointments should be kept to a minimum. Please do not cancel planned activities on a whim.

Now consider how you would feel, while reflecting on what King Solomon wrote — "we are once a man and twice a child," meaning some in their "winter season" do not easily adjust to unfavorable situations when they return to not being in control, consequently causing an unhappy experience in the lives of those around them. This doesn't give us reasons to forget or neglect shut-ins, especially family members and friends.

Check Before Bringing Food

What would hospitality be without a touch of sweet treats in the mix? While pondering that thought, keep in mind that many of the residents have dietary restrictions. Therefore, before preparing food items, contact the activity coordinator to get a clear understanding of the guidelines.

It is improper and unsafe to presume it is acceptable to share your favorite food items with the residents without first checking with the staff. The staff of most facilities recommends that if you wish to share food and other gifts with their residents, that it is discussed with them first. Once the guidelines are clear, it is our God-given responsibility to show respect for the health of others.

The recommended approach is to take your donation to the nurse's station and ask them to make the distribution because diets could have changed since your last conversation. "Hold on, I hear you," it is by faith that we believe our donation will go to the persons intended. To encourage proper and cheerful delivery, you might include the staff as recipients to your contribution.

Guidelines for Volunteering with Seniors

Did you know that one's life can be enriched by the experiences of seniors? Imagine how many valuable stories, lessons, and skills your elders can share with you. When you spend time volunteering with seniors, you will benefit personally as much as they do. You can gain treasured nuggets, too!

Here are some ways to lend a hand, a listening ear or your skills to seniors; by reminiscing or making new memories. Remember, just giving your time and conversation can often be the best gift.

Visiting Active Residents

One of the most meaningful things you can do for someone that is active is to share activities that they can relate to. Whether you're going to see a neighbor, loved one, or a new friend, make the most of your visit by planning ahead.

Call to schedule a time to drop by or get on the calendar for regular visits. Either way, the resident will look forward to seeing you. Bring a board game, cards, video, care package, or baked goods. Even if your schedule doesn't allow an extended visit, just a quick hello can brighten the person's day. The underlying message is, "I care and am thinking of you."

TIPS FOR VOLUNTEERING

Volunteering at a nursing home as a youth can be a wonderful experience. You will help your community and also accrue credits for scouts, school, or college. The residents of the home will be excited that you came. The following pointers will help you get started.

You will Need Permission

If you are a minor, you will need written permission from your parents or guardians to volunteer.

Choose Where to Volunteer

Go online to obtain the name and contact data of the nursing facility where you would like to volunteer.

Before You Call

Get a calendar and have a note pad ready to jot down information. Make sure the pen will write before you dial the number.

Making the Appointment

When someone answers say, "Hello, my name is_____, and I would like to volunteer at your facility. Can you give me the name and number of the person I need to speak with?" They will provide you with the name or transfer you to the department. Before you are transferred, say, "Thank you," and wait to be connected. Listen carefully in case there is a recording if it says to call back during a particular time, make a note and do so. Be prepared to leave your name and call back number, if asked to leave a voice-message.

Timely Contact

When they answer just say, "Hello, my name is_____, and I would like to volunteer." They will be happy for you to help and will give you instructions about what to do next. Again, make notes of any special instructions or information, including the name of the person you spoke with.

WHAT TO DO AS A VOLUNTEER

Follow Instructions

As a volunteer, it's vital to follow the rules and guidelines provided by the coordinator or other staff. Even if you think something can be done a better way, there is probably an important reason for the current system. Avoid causing problems or altering the schedule by following the rules of your assignment. You are there to serve, not to critique nor manage.

Go Above and Beyond

Following the rules and guidelines doesn't mean you have to do the bare minimum. If you're assigned to wheel patients from one room to another, take time with and talk to them along the way. Learn the names of those you interact with. Nothing is more important to a person than hearing their name. If the staff asks for your help, be willing to do so, even if it takes extra time or effort.

Choose Age Appropriate Activities

If you have the opportunity to plan an event, put yourself in the residents' shoes and consider what they will enjoy? If you're going to play music or karaoke, choose songs from their generation that they will recognize. Ask the residents or the staff what past activities have worked well and incorporate some of them into your plan. Even if it's not always an activity that you enjoy, remember that this isn't about you.

Be Consistent

If you say you'll be available for one hour every Wednesday morning, be consistent. Not only is it stressful for the staff and other volunteers if you miss your assignment, it can also be disappointing to the residents. Life at a nursing home can be mundane, so the residents really anticipate the visits and activities. Before committing to a volunteer schedule, make sure it's a consistent commitment that you can keep. If you ever need to adjust your schedule, give as much advance notice as possible. Before committing, always verify that you have dependable transportation, private or public.

My Experience: One day I went by the facility where our church conducts services to deliver some plants, and the assigned person wasn't there. The staff asked if I would fill-in to avoid the residents not having an activity during that time. Of course, I was glad to help out and had the time to do it.

Be Yourself

It can be intimidating at first because you may not know any of the residents. Keep in mind that not every person is the same. They have different personalities and interests, just like you. Act like you're meeting people your age and don't be afraid to be yourself. Tell them about your hobbies and interests and ask about theirs. Chances are, you might have more in common than you thought. Remember, they were your age once upon a time!

After volunteering at a healthcare facility, and realize that you are not adjusting to the program. Don't give up on helping others, consider finding out is there people in your community that need some help.

Start Local

There are people of various ages in our communities that would appreciate extra help in their homes. Sometimes their health prevents them from getting out and socializing. To help them not feel isolated, drop by for a visit, bring a meal, or share their favorite movie or television program. Research indicates that after dinner and the evening news most seniors will retire for the night; therefore, evening visits are highly recommended.

Offer to run errands for those who can't drive or must depend upon public transportation. Make it a weekly event when possible, and let them know they can call you when needed. You can also take them along as you run errands, so they can get out of the house and visit with you, at the same time.

It doesn't take a skilled handyman to do many around-the-house chores. Offer to rake leaves in the fall, shovel snow in the winter, plant flowers in the spring or fix little things around the house.

Be a Companion

If you don't have a parent or grandparent of your own that needs some extra care, there are plenty of seniors out there who could use some companionship and help! Some organizations can match you with the perfect new friend in your area.

- **Elder Helpers Program** allows you to sign up to help in ways that fit your interests and skills, from reading to handiwork.

- **Senior Companions** is a Senior Corps program for volunteers who are 55+. You can sign on to help older seniors with daily tasks, keeping them independent and in their own homes.

- **National Council on Aging** is another volunteer organization that assists seniors.

Continue Lifelong Learning

Whether you're at a nursing home, the neighbor's front porch, or loved one's home, ask yourself what you can learn from your elder friend. The depth and variety of their personal experiences may surprise you! While they've likely compiled stories over the years, it can often be challenging to know just what to ask to kick-start a conversation. Here are four ways to get started, as well as rekindle their memories and stories.

Discover their Passion

Does your friend love to cook? Ask them to share a favorite family recipe. Do they love to sing or draw? Get them to show you some of their earlier work. Did they serve in the military? Find what they're passionate about, and, chances are, they'll welcome the opportunity to chat for hours.

Ask about their Skills

If you don't already know about their career, ask questions about their accomplishments, lessons learned, or favorite memories. Please don't forget to ask about their hobbies aside from their profession. You may be amazed to learn that they will even offer to teach you their favorite techniques.

Log their Memories

Bring a journal or tablet and ask your friend to compile their memories. If they prefer you do the recording, of course, take advantage of the opportunity. You'll find it educational and rewarding to turn their stories in a documented history for posterity, and they will be flattered by your interest.

Make some Artwork

Turn their hand-picked pages of artwork into wall art. You may photocopy the best work and add a caption before mounting. The artwork will brighten their room, if in a facility, draw admiring comments from others.

TERMINAL CONDITIONS

Starting the Conversation

We're more likely to talk to our kids about safe sex and drugs than to talk to our parents about their final season of life plans. We tell ourselves it's too soon. Until one day we realize it's too late.

Nearly fifty percent of Americans say they would rely on family or friends to carry out their wishes about final life care; but most have never expressed those wishes. Some would want everything that medical technology has to offer. Others would opt for a gentle, pain-free death if their quality of life were seriously diminished. There's no right or wrong. Every person has the right to make that decision.

Research tells us that the best way to get others to discuss final days of care is to do so yourself. He or she suggests that you begin the decision-making process by asking yourself these what-if questions.

Terminal Conditions What-ifs

What if you had a terminal condition, and there was no reasonable possibility of recovery? What kind of treatments or life-saving measures would you consent to or refuse?

Unable to Make Decisions

What if you weren't able to make these decisions for yourself? Who would you want to make them for you?

Unable to Make Medical Decisions

What if your loved one needed to make those decisions for you? Does he or she know what you want?

Where to Have "The Conversation"

It is suggested to use family gatherings — wedding, anniversary, birthday, retirement, graduation, downsizing move, family holiday — to start the conversation.

Keep it light but heartfelt. You may start by letting your loved ones know your wishes, this could start a frank conversation among the generations about terminal illness, funeral plans, religious beliefs, and other end of life concerns.

ADVANCE DIRECTIVES FOR LGBT COUPLES

Love is Love

They love one another, they live together, and they care for each other in sickness and in health. In an emergency, they would want to be treated as a couple. They are each other's closest relative, the one who knows what the other's wishes are. But if you are lesbian, gay, bisexual or transgender and are hospitalized or unable to speak for yourself, who will be permitted to speak for you? Who will listen?

The following is good advice for anyone — sick or healthy, in a committed relationship or single, LGBT or straight. But it is particularly important for the lesbian, gay, bisexual or transgender person who has a terminal illness.

PET VISITS IN HOSPICE CARE

When Animals Do What People Can't

Remember *Lassie*? Each week on the 1950s television show the brave Collie saved her family and friends from wells, fires, and other dangers. The show demonstrated in dramatic fashion how hospice patients can benefit from the devotion of a four-legged friends.

Many hospice locations have pet visit volunteers who are trained to provide comfort and a special friendship to anyone who can benefit; from a child struggling to read, disaster victims or the elderly. Hospice pet volunteers visit patients in nursing homes, assisted living communities, and private homes.

Hospice pet visits offer a welcome distraction from illness and help people feel a little less lonely. They leave their patients smiling, more relaxed, and maybe even healthier. The therapeutic use of pets has gained more attention and widespread acceptance as it continues to bring measurable benefits to all kinds of needs.

Four Benefits of Pet Visits
Comfort care
Bringing back memories
Encourage activity
Providing unconditional love

MUSIC THERAPY FOR HOSPICE PATIENTS

Music therapy is more than a music activity in a nursing home or hospice facility. It is the clinical- and evidence-based use of music intervention by a board-certified music therapist. It assesses the strengths and needs of the patient and designs a plan of treatment that includes creating, singing, moving to, and/or listening to live, patient-preferred music within individual, group and/or family sessions.

Because music is non-threatening, enjoyable, and enhances brain function, people of diverse ages, cultures, and abilities can gain therapeutic benefits through music therapy. When offered to those at the final season of life, music therapy can bind with other healing energies to address the physical, emotional, mental, and social needs of hospice patients. While not appropriate for every hospice patient, music therapy can be surprisingly effective with an otherwise unresponsive patient.

Benefits

- Lack social interaction or sensory stimulation.
- Experience pain and symptoms that are difficult to control through traditional medical interventions.
- Feel anxious or affected by dementia.
- Look for a concrete way to cope, to define, and articulate feelings or thoughts.
- Face communication problems due to physical or intellectual impairments.
- Need spiritual support, possibly involving other family members.
- Enjoy music to enhance their quality of life or maintain dignity.

Techniques

Music therapists draw from an extensive array of music activities and interventions. For example, the therapist and patient might compose songs to help express feelings. A patient might learn to play the piano to improve fine motor skills or use musical instruments to cope with unspoken emotions.

Music Therapy Q and A

Q. Does the patient need prior training in music?

A. No. Symptoms, patient/family interest and response to a music therapy assessment determine whether music therapy is appropriate.

Q. Does the patient have to be alert and oriented to benefit from music therapy?

A. No. Music can trigger meaningful emotions and memories for disoriented patients, thereby improving communication, mood and quality of life.

Q. Will marginally responsive patients be able to hear the music?

A. Hearing is thought to be one of the last active senses, so music therapy may be quite appropriate for unresponsive patients.

Q. Should music therapy be private?

A. At times, privacy may be necessary. But generally, family participation is actively encouraged to enhance the connection between loved ones.

Q. Can all patients benefit from music therapy?

A. While beneficial for many patients, music can increase agitation and anxiety in others. Not every patient and family will be interested in music therapy. Music therapists are trained in assessment and will never continue therapy if a patient displays a negative or harmful response

TELECARE 24/7 ACCESS TO HOSPICE CARE

Available Evenings, Weekends and Holidays

Telecare service is your reassurance that you have a direct line to medical advice, support and hands-on care, as needed; at any time of the day or night. During weekdays, you contact your hospice team at the number they provide. But when your hospice team is off duty, your Telecare hospice team is available evenings, weekends, and holidays.

A Telecare nurse or other patient care expert answers your call. He or she has access to your files and the expertise to answer your questions, contact your physician or dispatch an on-call team member to the bedside — whether it's 5:45pm on Monday, or midnight on New Year's Eve. Telecare is there for you, and your love one.

> *"When we have done our best,*
> *we should wait the result in peace."*
> *J. Lubbock*

Final Earthly Planning

COURSES OF ACTION

Just as the aging process is part of the Almighty's plan, so is physical death. No matter how prepared we think we are, when the time comes, most of us will realize that we are not as ready as we thought. That leads us to some courses of action that will help us through the last earthly season of our families, friends, and ultimately ourselves.

Before we address our courses of action, we must remember that the pain of the loss of a loved one will vary, depending on several personal and external factors.

Let's consider my experiences: my brother was sixteen living at home when he transitioned. Of the five siblings, two were living out of state, while most of the other relatives were nearby, making contact mostly word of mouth. When my father departed at the age of eighty-four, my mother had already made her transition, and all of the siblings were living out of state, with grandchildren out of the Country. The notification process of contact was very different and extensive.

Once the funeral director has been contacted, a time is set to meet and make arrangements for the services of the deceased. The total expenses should include the eulogist and the musician, who will be paid by the funeral director.

Before and during the home-going activities there are several things to consider. Here are some areas where one should offer their assistance:

- Make yourself available for a specific time to answer the phone and greet visitors or answer inquiries. This person should be knowledgeable of the family's plans and activities, including the address of friends' homes that may be used by the out of town guest, as well as any special needs of the family.

- Speak on behalf of the family only in the areas where they have asked you to do so. Know the name of the family member in charge before you begin your assignment; this will prevent unnecessary interruptions later. Also, ask for a written itinerary of planned events and family's schedule, if applicable.

- Part of your phone duties could include notifying others of the person's departure; if you are not comfortable with this, please advise the person in charge prior to making the first call. One never wants to increase the grief of others by sharing their own emotions while making a call.

- The spouse and close family members will need help with personal decisions, including apparel for before, during and after the services. The amount of assistance necessary will depend on their emotional and/ or physical conditions at the time.

- Phone messages should be written on a closeable book like notebook or diary that is kept near the phone. This will provide easy access for the family and others that will be filling that duty. If you record it on your electronic device, it will leave when you do. Each message should include the caller's name, relationship to the family, contact information, date and time of the call, along with the message. The same applies to the visitors. For privacy, the note book should be closed when not in use.

- Written condolences, gifts, and food items should be put in a specific place, as instructed by the family. Do not open or unwrap items without permission from the family member in charge. If the items are in a container that should be returned to the giver, mark it clearly with their name (without being obvious) making a note in the record book by the person's name including a contact number.

Non-Traditional Giving

Forms of giving may also be non-traditional and much appreciated by most families. When making your choice, consider the following:

- Gift cards or postage stamps.
- Treating the spouse or next of kin to a meal several weeks after the service - send a card stating your desire including contact information.

- Running errands or house sitting during the services and or while the family is out of town. Of course, house sitting would only apply to close trusted friends or relatives.

- Performing house or yard work, behind the scene before, during and after the services.

- Caring for pets or children.

- Visit or contact the survivor in the days following the service.

- Groceries, laundry or dry cleaning help is very helpful, not only during the immediate loss, but in the following weeks, depending on the survivors' circumstances.

My Experience: *My father was blind, and we had to contact a caregiver and make physical changes in the home. With those changes in place, he lived there nine years with the help of the caregiver, and friends.*

- Visiting or keeping in contact on special days, including the anniversary day of the loved one's departure, other anniversaries, birthdays, vacation times, and holidays, all of which can be difficult for the surviving spouse.

- Help prepare Thank You notes or correspondence following a loved one's departure. If you have legible handwriting, consider offering help. It will be much appreciated.

- Volunteer or assign someone to coordinate transportation and housing for out of town guests.

- Make a list of the names, mode of transportation and time of arrival.

- Verify the name and address of the hotel to be recommended or utilized, there may be more than one in the area with the same or similar name.

- Be specific when stating the dates and times of your availability.

Obituaries!

What are they, and what purpose do they serve concerning the final service of a person's life? Think of it this way; it is the last written expression of the deceased's personal and family data, as well as accomplishments.

To ensure that an obituary is complete and accurate, one should consider writing an outline of their obit. This is not a guarantee that what you write will be your final story, but it will give the person in charge of telling your story some useful facts and references.

Your notes don't have to be professionally prepared, but should be typed or clearly legible and in a location known to your family member or friend. During one of my family reunions, part of the activities was to prepare a draft for both of our parent's final services. Each sibling was given a copy to review later and asked to send any changes to the oldest sibling. She was in charge of preparing the obit at the time of our parents transitioning. Not expecting to need the information for years to come, we were surprised, but prepared when we had to write our mother's final obit fifteen months later.

Should you chose to make collecting the story a group project, it's less stressful when the family member is in good health and can contribute. One must also expect challenges from some of those present. Everyone doesn't perceive the importance in the same way. The assigned person should attempt to reiterate the purpose, and remind them that this is just a guideline for the future. If they do not want to participate, so be it.

Areas to Include

- Newspaper articles about the person.

  _____

  _____

  _____

- Copy of recognition from an employer, community and church accomplishments.

  _____

  _____

  _____

- Favorite songs, Bible scripture, readings, pictures, and favorite sayings.

  _____

  _____

  _____

- Favorite places of travel, sports interest, childhood adventures, accomplishments or challenges.

  _____

  _____

  _____

- Parting words to the family, close friend, and children are all part of your story.

  _____

  _____

  _____

- Names of family, friends, and associates are to be included.

_____

_____

_____

Include stories about their sense of humor or wit.

_____

_____

_____

- The survivors should be listed with the next of kin first.

_____

_____

_____

- The children's parent should be listed if separated from the deceased.

_____

_____

_____

The Sequence of Events

- Name of deceased, city, state and date of birth and date of passing, parents names and educational accomplishments.

_____

_____

_____

- Accomplishments related to the Kingdom of God, then the professional world.

_____

_____

_____

- List the survivors first and then those that preceded them in death.

_____

_____

_____

Newspaper Articles and Expenses

There are two forms of notices: One is written by a newspaper staff person or submitted by the funeral homes or crematoriums, which are part of the funeral expenses. People often wonder why the family didn't put more information in the newspaper about their loved one. The newspaper charges per line including the obit and photograph. The price may range from $ 200.00 to $ 500.00 depending on the length of the obit and related information. When placing the notice in a big city paper, the cost can be up to $ 75.00 per line.

It does sound expensive; however, unless a person is well-known, this will be the last public notice about them. Let's get it all out there, to the extent resources allow. This is our parting tribute to the deceased.

The Program

The family or close friends usually prepare the program of the deceased. One must keep in mind the time constraints of the family, the funeral home and final resting place.

Traditional Services

- Musical Selection

  _____

  _____

  _____

- Greetings

  _____

  _____

  _____

- Scriptures

  _____

  _____

  _____

- Prayer

  _____

  _____

  _____

- Musical Selection

  _____

  _____

  _____

- Remarks by selected people and/or clergy

  _____

  _____

  _____

- Resolutions

_____

_____

_____

- Obituary reading (audible or silent)

_____

_____

_____

- Musical Selection

_____

_____

_____

- Words of comfort and life accomplishments (Eulogy)

_____

_____

_____

- Recessional instructions

_____

_____

_____

- Departing musical selection

_____

_____

_____

Non-Traditional Services
- Musical Selections
- Welcome
- Expressions by Friends
- Expressions by Family
- Poems/Readings
- Musical Selections

Gathering of Friends

- The location and time to share memories of the deceased will be announced.

- There will not be a specific structure for the event.

Additional Information

- The Pallbearers (often grandsons or special friends of the family)

- Flower Bearers (names or organization they represent)

- Family Acknowledgement

_____

_____

_____

- Special Thanks from the Family

_____

_____

_____

- Final arrangements entrusted to

_____

_____

_____

- Internment

_____

_____

_____

- Repast location

_____

_____

_____

Repast and Locations

The repast is a time to continue celebrating the life of the decease in a relaxed atmosphere. It will also give friends that couldn't attend the other services the opportunity to come by. The repast is optional during the final ceremonies. Family time constraints and funds are sometimes the deciding factors. A private or public repast can also be scheduled at a later date. The attendees usually are immediate family and invited guests.

The menu varies from a sit-down meal to light refreshments. Friends usually prepare the food. The cost isn't typically part of the funeral expenses. However, it could be depending on the facility. The repast for my parents was held at a church where they weren't members.

The family paid for the food and rental of the building. When a member is in good standing there isn't usually a charge for the repast.

Music, flowers and a collage with the accomplishment and life events may be on display during the meal.

- Church Fellowship Halls
- Senior Centers
- Community Centers
- Restaurants — private room
- Outdoor Pavilions
- Appropriate Resident of Family Member or Friend

SONGS — READINGS AND SCRIPTURES

Choosing the right song can be challenging if you didn't personally know the deceased. Be safe and check with immediate family first. If they have no preference, you may choose ones that you have heard before, or ask the funeral director for suggestions. Here's a list of several options that are commonly used.

Love Songs
"Take My Breath Away" by Irving Berlin
"Coming Around Again" by Carly Simon
"Together Again" by Janet Jackson
"You Raise Me Up" by Josh Groban

Sentimental Songs
"Wind beneath My Wing" by Bette Midler
"Time after Time" by Cindy Lauper
"May it Be, and Only Time" by Enya
"I'll be There" by Escape Club
"The Dance" by Garth Brooks

Songs for the Death of a Spouse
"Memories, and The Way We Were" by Barbra Streisand
"Because You Loved Me, and My Heart will Go On" by Celine
  Dion

Golden Oldies
"Wonderful World" by Louis Armstrong
"Unforgettable" by Nat King Cole
"Every Grain of Sand" by Bob Dylan
"Farewell My Friend" by Dennis Wilson
"My Way" by Elvis Presley
"The Last Waltz" by Engelbert Humperdink

Rock Songs
"In Loving Memory" by Alter Bridge
"Change" by Black Sabbath
"Hallelujah" by Bon Jovi
"Turn- Turn-Turn" by the Byrds

Popular Songs
"To Where You Are" by Josh Groban
"Ave Maria" by Sarah Brightman
"In the Arms of an Angel" by Sarah Mclaghlan

Religious Songs
"The Prayer" by Celine Dion
"Spirit in the Sky" by Gareth Gates
"My Sweet Lord" by George Harrison
"Amazing Grace" by Judy Collins & the Choir
"Amazing Grace" by LeAnn Rimes
"The Lord Is My Shepherd" by Mormon Tabernacle Choir

Some of the Most Loved Hymns

"Amazing Grace" by Virginia Harmony
"It Is Well with My Soul" by Philip Bliss
"The Old Rugged Cross" by George Bennard
"Blessed Assurance" by Phoebe Palmer Knapp
"The Lord's Prayer" by Albert Hay Malotte
"When We All Get to Heaven" by Emily D. Wilson
"Brighter Day Ahead" by C. Walker
"All the Way My Saviour Leads Me" by Crosby-Lowry
"A Charge to Keep I Have" by Wesley-Mason
"Great Is Thy Faithfulness" by Chisolm-Gould
"Jesus Savior Pilot Me" by Hooper-Gould
"My Faith Looks Up To Thee" by Palmer-Mason
"What a Friend We Have in Jesus" by Scriver-Converse

POEMS

"God Saw You Getting Tired" Author Unknown
"I'm Free" by Janice M. Fair-Salters
"Miss Me But Let Me Go" by Janice M. Fair-Salters

"Crossing the Bar" by Alfred Lord Tennyson
"Don't Cry" Anonymous
"Life's Secret Story" by Sally Pipkin

"A Heart of Gold" Author Unknown
"The Final Fight" —Anonymous
"A Mother's Farwell to Her Children" by Helen Steiner Rice

"His Journey Just Begun" —Anonymous
"The Serenity Prayer" by Reinhold Niebuhr
"Thou Leadest Me" Author Unknown
"We Will Miss You" Anonymous

READINGS FROM THE HOLY SCRIPTURES

Psalm Twenty-Three
Psalm Eight
John Chapter Fourteen select verses

II Timothy Chapter Four verses seven and eight
Isaiah Chapter Forty-One verse ten
Psalm Ninety-One verses one to eleven

II Corinthians Chapter Five verse eight
John Chapter Eleven verses twenty-five and twenty-six
Proverbs Chapter Thirty-One verses twenty-five to thirty-one

Psalm 27 verses four, five – thirteen, fourteen
Revelations Chapter Twenty-One verse four

SCRIPTURE READINGS FOR SPECIFIC AGES

For A Child

As a father shows compassion to his children, so the Lord shows compassion to those who fear him. For he knows our frame; he remembers that we are dust, As for man, his days are like grass; he flourishes like a flower of the field; for the wind passes over it, and it is gone, and its place knows it no more. But the steadfast love of the Lord is from everlasting to everlasting on those who fear him, and his righteousness to children's children, to those who keep his covenant and remember to do his commandments (Psalm 103:13-18 ESV).

At that time the disciples came to Jesus, saying. Who is the greatest in the kingdom of heaven? And calling to him a child, he put him in the midst of them and said, Truly, I say to you, unless you turn and become like children, you will never enter the kingdom of heaven. Whoever humbles himself like this child is the greatest in the kingdom of heaven. Whoever receives one such child in my name receives me, but whoever causes one of these little ones who believe in me to sin, it would be better for him to have a great millstone fastened around his neck and to be drowned in the depth of the sea. (Matthew 18:1-6 ESV).

Then children were brought to him that he might lay his hands on them and pray. The disciples rebuked the people, but Jesus said, Let the little children come to me and do not hinder them, for to such belongs the kingdom of heaven. And he laid his hands on them and went away. (Matthew 19: 13-15 ESV).

Grace to you and peace from God our Father and the Lord Jesus Christ. Blessed be the God and Father of our Lord Jesus Christ, the Father of mercies and God of all comfort, who comforts us in all our affliction, so that we may be able to comfort those who are in any affliction, with the comfort with which we ourselves are comforted by God. For as we share abundantly in Christ's sufferings, so through Christ we share abundantly in comfort too. If we are afflicted, it is for your comfort and salvation; and if we are comforted, it is for your comfort, which you experienced when you patiently endure the same suffering that we suffer. Our hope for you is unshaken, for we know that as you share in our suffering, you will also share in our comfort. (II Corinthians 1:2-7 ESV).

For A Youth

How can a young man keep his way pure? By guarding it according to your word. With my whole heart I seek you; let me not wander from your commandments! I have stored up your word in my heart that I might not sin against you. Blessed are you, O Lord; teach me your statures. (Psalm 119:9-12 ESV)!

The glory of young men is their strength. (Proverbs 20:29 ESV).

Rejoice, O young man, in your youth, and let your heart cheer you in the days of your youth. Walk in the ways of your heart and the sight of your eyes. But know that for all these things God will bring you into judgement. Remove vexation from your heart, and put away pain from your body, for youth and the dawn of life are vanity. (Ecclesiastes 11:9-10 ESV).

Remember also your Creator in the days of your youth, before the evil days come and the years draw near of which you will say I have no pleasure in them; and the dust returns to the earth as it was, and the spirit returns to God who gave it. (Ecclesiastes 12: 1, 7 ESV).

The Mature Person

But concerning that day or that hour, no one knows, not even the angles in heaven, nor the Son, but only the Father. Be on guard, keep awake. For you do not know when the time will come. It is like a man going on a journey, when he leaves home and puts his servants in charge, each with his work, and commands the doorkeeper to stay awake. Therefore stay awake — for you do not know when the master of the house will come, in the evening, or at midnight, or when the rooster crows, or in the morning — lest he come suddenly and find you asleep. And what I say to you I say to all; stay awake. (Mark 13:32-37 ESV).

But be doers of the word, and not hearers only, deceiving yourselves. For if anyone is a hearer of the word and not a doer, he is like a man who looks intently at his natural face in a mirror. For he looks at himself and goes away and at once forgets what he was like. But the one who looks into the perfect law, the law of liberty, and perseveres, being no hearer who forgets but a doer who acts, he will be blessed in his doing. (James 1: 22-25 ESV).

The Aged

Man who is born of woman is of few days and full of trouble. He comes forth like a flower and fades away; He flees like a shadow and does not continue. (Job 14:1-2).

The days of our lives are seventy years; and if by reason of strength they are eighty years, yet their boast is only labor and sorrow; for it is soon cut off, and we fly away. So teach us to number our days that we may gain a heart of wisdom. And let the beauty of the Lord our God be upon us, and establish the work of our hands for us; Yes, establish the work of our hands. (Psalm 90:10, 12, 17).

The silver-haired head is a crown of glory, if it is found in the way of righteousness. He who is slow to anger is better than the mighty, and he who rules his spirit than he who takes a city. (Proverbs 16:31-32).

... and the time of my departure is at hand. I have fought the good fight, I have finished the race, I have kept the faith. Finally there is laid up for me the crown of righteousness, which the Lord, the righteous Judge, will give to me on that Day, and not to me only but also to all who have loved His appearing. (II Timothy 4: 6-8).

Blessed are the dead who die in the Lord from now on, that they rest from their labors, and their works follow them. (Revelation 14:13).

General Scriptures

The Lord is my shepherd; I shall not want. He makes me to lie down in green pastures; He leads me besides the still waters. He restores my soul; He leads me in the paths of righteousness For His name's sake. Yea, though I walk through the valley of the shadow of death, I will fear no evil; for You are with me; Your rod and Your staff, they comfort me. You prepare a table before me in the presence of my enemies; you anoint my head with oil; my cup runs over. Surely goodness and mercy shall follow me all the days of my life; and I will dwell in the house of the Lord Forever. (Psalm 23:1-6).

Because you have made the Lord, who is my refuse, Even the Most High, your habitation, No evil shall befall you, nor shall any plague come near your dwelling; for He shall give His angels charge over you, To keep you in all your ways. They shall bear you up in their hands. (Psalm 91: 9-12).

I will lift up my eyes to the hill — from whence comes my help? My help comes from the Lord, Who made heaven and earth. He will not allow your foot to be moved; He who keeps you will not slumber. Behold, He who keeps Israel Shall neither slumber nor sleep, The Lord is your keeper; The Lord is your shade at your right hand. The sun shall not strike you by day, nor the moon by night. The Lord shall preserve you from all evil; He shall preserve your soul. The Lord shall preserve you're going out and your coming in from this time forth, and even forevermore. (Psalm 121: 1-8).

Let not your heart be troubled; you believe in God, believe also in Me. In My Father's house are many mansions; if it were not so, I would have told you. I go to prepare a place for you. And if I go and prepare a place for you, I will come again and receive you to myself; that where I am, there you may be also. And where I go you know, and the way you know. Thomas said to Him, Lord we do not know where you are going, and how can we know the way? Jesus said to him, I am the way, the truth, and the life. No one comes to the Father except through Me. If you had known Me, you would have known My Father also; and from now on you know Him and have seen Him. Peace I leave with you, My peace I give to you; not as the world gives do I give to you. Let not your heart be troubled, neither let it be afraid. (John 14: 1-7, 27).

My brethren, count it all joy when you fall into various trials, knowing that the testing of your faith produces patience. But let patience have its perfect work, that you may be perfect and complete, lacking nothing. Blessed is the man who endures temptation; for when he has been proved, he will receive the crown of life which the Lord has promised to those who love him. (James 1:1-2, 12).

Benediction Scriptures

The Lord bless you and keep you; The Lord make His face shine upon you, and be gracious to you; The Lord lift up His countenance upon you, And give you peace. (Numbers 6:24-26).

God be merciful to us and bless us, and cause His face to shine upon us. That Your way may be known on earth, Your salvation among all nations. (Psalm 67: 1-2).

The grace of the Lord Jesus Christ, and the love of God, and the communion of the Holy Spirit be with you all, Amen. (II Corinthians 13:14).

And the peace of God, which surpasses all understanding, will guard your hearts and minds through Christ Jesus. The grace of our Lord Jesus Christ be with you all. Amen. (Philippians 4:7, 23).

Now may the God of peace who brought up our Lord Jesus from the dead, that great Shepherd of the sheep, through the blood of the everlasting covenant, make you complete in every good work to do His will, working in you what is well pleasing in His sight, through Jesus Christ, to whom be glory forever and ever. Amen. (Hebrews 13: 20-21).

Now to Him who is able to keep you from stumbling, And to present you faultless before the presence of His glory with exceeding joy, To God our Savior, Who alone is wise, be glory and majesty, Dominion and power, Both now and forever. Amen. (Jude 24-25).

THE EULOGY

A eulogy is somewhat like a personalized speech. It is given at a funeral as a testimonial to the life of the deceased, and to encourage the living. It is usually given by a clergy, relative or a close personal friend of the person who passed away.

Eulogy Preparation

- Mention some of the accomplishments of the deceased.
- Put your key thoughts in writing.
- Remember to encourage the living.
- Be prepared in case of an emergency.

PALLBEARER PROTOCOL

Caskets can be quite heavy, so make sure all of the pallbearers are capable of carrying and lifting. They may have to walk over uneven ground, female pallbearers should wear comfortable shoes and clothing that enables ease of movement.

For people who have chosen cremation, a traditional pallbearer is not necessary. However, you can choose honorary pallbearers who walk alongside and behind the person carrying the urn with the ashes.

Tips

When someone asks you to be a pallbearer, it means that he or she has confidence in you.

- Accept the honor and responsibility if at all possible.
- Understand what an honor this is. Handle it with respect and dignity.
- Arrive at the funeral service location on time or early if requested.
- If you can't control your emotions, decline to serve.

CREMATION AND MEMORIAL SERVICES

Cremation Services

The total expenses for a cremation service should be less than that of a traditional funeral. During the service the remains of the deceased may be in a casket or urn. Depending on the preference of the time of cremation. The order of service usually follow that of a traditional service.

Memorial Services

The order of service usually follow that of a traditional funeral. The date of the service may be several months after the deceased has passed. It is held at the convenience of the family in a location that the deceased loved, or that the majority of the family visited often. A picture of the love one is usually on display during the service.

CULTURAL FLORAL ARRANGEMENTS

Appropriate or Not

During final services, each culture and faith's traditions regarding flowers vary. When unsure whether flowers are suitable, check with local religious leaders or member of the immediate family. Here are some general guidelines.

Baha'i - Flowers are appropriate.

Buddhist - Flowers are appropriate.

Catholic - Flowers are usually welcomed and appreciated. For deliveries to the church the florist will contact the parish for details. Practices may vary concerning casket sprays and other displays.

Church of Jesus Christ of Latter Day Saints — the Mormons - Flowers arranged on a cross or crucifix are inappropriate. Other floral tributes are acceptable.

Eastern Orthodox - There is often an emphasis on white flowers. You may send them to the funeral home. Those unable to attend the funeral may send flowers to the funeral home or the residence of the departed.

Other Christian Faiths - Floral arrangements are an expression of love, whether a traditional, memorial, or cremation service. Fruit and food baskets are becoming more popular in lieu of flower arrangements. These and similar items should be sent to the residence and not to the location of the service.

Hindu - Flowers aren't necessarily part of the Hindu tradition; however, they are appropriate. The arrangements should consist of garlands and mixed seasonal sprays of flowers.

Islamic - The suitability of sending flowers varies; the Islamic emphasis on simplicity makes flowers by tradition unsuitable. If you are unsure, ask the opinion of the local religious leaders or the family. When flowers are requested, roses or other aromatic varieties would be excellent. You may also place palm branches, other greenery, or individual flowers at the final resting site.

Jewish - During the mourning period, fruit and food are sent to the home instead of flowers. Modern traditions are generally not practiced among Orthodox Jews. Friends of the deceased often choose to send flowers to bereaved family members at their home. It's also becoming common to have some floral decorations sent to adorn the synagogue foyer.

TRADITIONAL ARRANGEMENTS

Throughout history, flowers have been an essential part of final services. After family, friends, and the eulogy, flowers are considered next among those who have lost a family member as the most meaningful aspect of funerals. They give needed respite to the family, a subject of light conversation by guests, and an atmosphere brightener during a somber time.

Flowers show admiration for the departed, as well as loving support of the family, especially when you cannot be there in person.

Spray - Flowers designed for viewing from one side only, and placed on an easel.

Wreath - A floral presentation in the form of a circle illustrating the continuing life cycle.

Cut Arrangements - Fresh flowers of various types in a vase, basket or another container, sometimes including live plants. These also may include a display of the deceased's favorite hobby.

Casket Spray - Usually ordered by the family, and consisting of the deceased and or families favorite flowers.

Inside Piece - A small floral design for placement inside the casket; sometimes on a satin heart-shaped pillow or in the hands of the beloved.

When selecting an arrangement for the home you may want to consider: bud vase, table arrangement, potted plants or live shrub. Waterless plants are also fitting for the services or the home.

When a Charity is suggested- is Sending Flowers Appropriate?

Yes! Flowers are considered by most to be a suitable expression of kindness, in conjunction with your gift to your favorite charity. If the family requests contributions to a specific charity or cause in lieu of flowers, this should be given significant consideration; either in place of or addition to flowers.

Arrangement with a Special Meaning

Ask the florist to put the arrangement in a special container, using flowers that represent the personality, your relationship with, or a hobby/ special interest of the deceased. For example, if the person traveled extensively, ask for a container in the shape or name of the places they visited, or consider something that represents their profession or sports-related activity. A gavel for a judge will work.

Identifying a Group Arrangement

To identify each individual's participation, put his or her favorite flower in a fresh arrangement; otherwise, they will be represented by their name on the card. The size of the arrangement should be representative of the number of names on the card. A contact name and address should also be provided for convenience of the family. The group may consist of: relatives, friends, church family, co-workers, neighbors, or professional organization.

Right or Wrong Arrangement

Sympathy and funeral flowers protocol isn't an area that most people focus on; however, when the need arises, and knowledge is limited you may find the following tips helpful.

There isn't a right or wrong arrangement. The best way to decide is by selecting something you think the family will enjoy during and after the services. When you are choosing cut flowers, try to include the family's or the deceased's favorite flower. My Father's favorite flower was the yellow rose; during the services each family member wore a yellow rose.

Boutonnieres and Corsages are non-traditional ways to give flowers that will last during and after the services. Before this idea is considered it's recommended to check with the family.

Flowers for Cremation Services

An arrangement that can be enjoyed in the residence after the service or ask the florist or family for suggestions.

Contributions after the Funeral Services

Yes! Contributions are in order; send food, gift or fruit basket to the home with a personal note of condolences. Other expressions are always in order, such as an invitation to dinner; attend their favorite sports event or an event of their choice.

Choosing the Right Arrangement

It is reassuring to know that this is one time when you do not have to be the expert. That is the responsibility of the florist. State your situation and their representative will guide you through the process. They will lead you through each step, from the budget to the type of arrangements, delivery date and time, as well as non- traditional options that are available. They will also coordinate delivery to the home or service site, if you prefer.

Notes and Cards

You choose not to send traditional expressions, but would like to send a card. Should it be sent before, during or after the services? Cards and or notes are acceptable before, during and after the formal service.

Receiving cards creates an additional time for the family to gather and reflect on what their loved one meant to others, and the impact they had on their lives. Your name and contact information should be included on the card or note.

Reading the cards in remembrances of their loved one brings comfort to the family in the days following the services.

VISITING TIMES

With modern technology, some people are choosing to sign the guest register online and not visit the funeral home or location of the service.

This is a matter of personal choice and is proper even if you visit the physical location.

If you decide to attend the visitation, funeral, or graveside service, the length of your visit is a matter of preference.

If the facility is crowded you may shorten your visit, and visit the family later. When visiting, regardless of the location, use your "inside voice."

FUNERAL HOME THERAPY DOG — HUMAN COMFORT

During the loss of a loved one comfort is one of the things we need most. Now "a man's best friend" therapy dogs have been added to the list. They are trained in obedience, given a name tag and the specific breed is chosen because of their personality. They are assigned a particular seat and will remain seated until ordered to move by the person-in-charge.

Benefits of a Therapy Dog:
- Give an atmosphere of home to dog lovers.
- Give a restless child a friend to play with.
- An encourager when more than a hug is needed.
- A conversation changer during an awkward moment.
- A comforter for all ages.

Therapy dogs are trained to pick out the person that is really hurting. They will interact with that person by sitting by their feet without making sounds.

Comfort Others in Love — Your Season Will Come
by Helen Rogers

FUNERAL ATTIRE — WEAR OR NOT TO WEAR

You heard that a family member, friend, co-worker, neighbor or someone you know has made their earthly transition. Based on your relationship to the departed, you send flowers or other condolences. The next step is deciding the proper attire.

Consider These Tips

What is my relationship to the deceased? If you answer immediate family, the family member in charge will tell all the members what the colors or special distinction will be.

For Example: *for my father's service the family wore a yellow rose. For my cousin, all the females wore hats in her memory.*

Sometimes the entire family will wear black or white. Other times the adults will wear black or navy blue and the younger children will wear white or ivory outfits. Personal situations and financial circumstances should always be considered.

When you are a friend of the deceased, make it easy on yourself and wear dark hues ranging from olive green to navy with a soft accent piece.

If you are unsure about the culture, select an outfit on the conservative side. Make a mental note while you are there and apply it should the need arise in the future.

If you attend the visitation only, your attire should represent the occasion (somber yet warm) and not the fact that you are coming from the office on casual Friday, or some other event. However, it is not as formal as attending the final service. The same applies when visiting the family at the home of the deceased.

There are quite a few myths about funerals that you don't need to worry about. The most important thing to remember is that you should never call attention to yourself with your outfit.

Be Conservative

You will probably want to avoid a bright floral dress or wild print or neon necktie, unless the family of the deceased asks you to. It is also not appropriate to show too much skin, so don't wear something with a plunging neckline.

Women — Not to Wear

Avoid mini-skirts, low-cut blouses or dresses, and spandex. You don't want to draw attention to yourself.

Women may wear skirts and blouses, dresses, or pantsuits that don't emphasize your curves, cleavage, or too much leg.

Keep your accessories simple. You may find yourself walking in the grass or on uneven ground, so leave your stilettos for other events, and wear more sensible flats or low-heeled shoes. Don't wear a floppy hat that's meant for a day at the beach. Jewelry should be understated, choose it with care.

Men — Not to Wear

Men shouldn't wear sports caps or any head-gear with writing on it. Leave your printed T-shirts in the drawer and opt for something more subtle and conservative. Don't add a vibrant printed tie, unless there is a reason to do otherwise. A conservative suit or tailored pants and a blazer are appropriate for most traditional funerals.

Exceptions

There are exceptions to the above. It is acceptable to dress in a military uniform for the funeral of a veteran. If your religion or the religion of the deceased calls for a specific style of attire, follow the rules.

Many people consider funerals a celebration of life rather than a sad end-of-life occasion. If this is the case, the family of the deceased may ask people to dress in a more upbeat manner. Honor their request.

Fifteen Wardrobe Considerations

1. This is not the time or place to show off your sexiest outfit.

2. You shouldn't wear anything that requires constant adjusting.

3. Your jewelry should be simple and understated.

4. Follow the dress code for the church if the funeral service is being held in the sanctuary.

5. If you are unsure how to dress, think about what you would wear to an office job interview and wear that.

6. Ladies may wear a sleeveless dress with a tailored jacket, sweater, or shawl with it.

7. You don't have to go out and buy a new outfit. Remember that a nice jacket can complete your outfit and make it funeral ready.

8. Don't wear anything that makes noise. The clinging sound of stacked bangle bracelets is disruptive and shows a lack of respect for the occasion.

9. If the family request more festive attire, you may wear bright colors.

10. Keep your makeup to a minimum. If you have a tendency to cry at funerals, make sure your mascara is waterproof.

11. If you have tattoos that may offend others, cover them up.

12. Sunglasses are appropriate for outdoor funerals. The plainer the better.

13. Keep your hairstyle as simple and natural as possible.

14. Don't wear strong perfume or scented body lotions. Some people are highly allergic, and you don't want to cause others to become ill during the services.

15. For any occasion your outfit is important, including funerals, and should not cause unnecessary drama and embarrassment

CONVERSATIONS OF
DO'S AND DON'TS — BECAUSE

Do Say

    I'm sorry about your loss.

    Give the person/family the opportunity to talk about the transitioned member.

    Be a good listener while they share their memories, shed tears with them if necessary.

    When speaking about the deceased, use their name; it gives an affectionate touch to the conversation.

    Assure the person/family that grieving is a normal reaction to the home-going of a loved one.

    After the person/family have expressed their feeling, pause and ask how you may help.

Don't Say

    I know how you feel. Expressed with strong emotions.

Because

    Is it really possible to know exactly how another feels?

Don't say

    You'll get over your loss real soon.

Because

    Time alone does not heal the pain.

Don't say

    At least he or she is in a better place.

Because

    That statement does not allow the grieving process to take place and will cause an unnecessary delay in healing.

Don't say

    Your baby is in heaven, you know.

Because

    One's faith in the eternal home for babies doesn't remove the pain of the lost.

Don't say
    At least they were not alert during their latter days when speaking to someone in the decease age range.
Because
    This is an observation on your part that doesn't ease the loss of the bereaved; just because a person is unable to speak about it doesn't always mean they can't understand what is going on around them.

Don't say
    He or she had a good life. Why are you so sad?
Because
    This statement is suggesting that the degree of grief is based on the lifestyle of the person.

Don't say
    Say or have the expectation that things will be back to normal in little or no time.
Because
    It is not fair to put a limit on others grieving time period. The departed will never be replaced, so normal is not possible in the life of the survivors.

Don't say
    You have grieved long enough, don't you think it's time to get on with your life.
Because
    There is no set time limit for a person to grieve, however, there should be a decline in the severity of the pain with time.

Don't say
    He or she was just a baby, how could you be that attached.
Because
    You are making a judgmental statement; the intimacy of a relationship varies with each individual.

Don't say
>She was old — no one lives forever you know.

Because
>No matter the age, the loss of the person has left a void in the life of the family.

Don't say
>He or she was just a friend.

Because
>Regardless of the relationship, a loss is still painful.

Don't say
>Did you expect them to live forever?

Because
>Experiencing hurt and a sense of loss is part of the grieving process.

Don't say
>Dry your eyes, you know your loved one would be upset if they knew you were still crying.

Because
>You are trying to equate the pain of the present with the possible emotions of the past.

Now that you have reviewed the "do's, don'ts and because list"; consider these four easy to remember tips to eliminate embarrassment for those you are attempting to comfort.

1. Use your best listening skills at all times.
2. Exercise understanding using verbal and nonverbal expressions.
3. Limit your feedback; just be a good listener.
4. Make yourself available as the need arises without being pushy.

"Tomorrow, is the first blank page of a 365 page book. Write a good one." – Brad Paisley

Children and Adults Coping with Grief

CHILDREN'S EXPRESSIONS OF GRIEF

Decades ago death was a natural part of a child's life. Grandparents often lived with the families, so children witnessed them growing older and dying. Modern medicine has made strides in reducing mortality and has prolonged life expectancy for the elderly. Therefore, children witness fewer deaths. With the increasing numbers of health care facilities, more elderly die outside the home environment. However, children still need to be taught about death and grief.

Research has proven that children have the ability to experience and express grief, but it is often drawn out over a longer period of time than that of an adult.

The grieving process helps people heal from their loss. Pain is a natural reaction when we lose someone close, and children are capable of accepting painful reality directly and openly. When adults try to protect children from the pain of loss, it is usually themselves they are trying to protect.

The most important thing to remember in helping children cope with the death of a loved one is to allow them to express their grief in their own way and in their own time. The parent should not pressure children to resume their normal activities if they are not ready.

Children tend to have grief moments followed by normal activities. Children may not be able to concisely verbalize what they are feeling and instead may demonstrate their feelings through their behavior. They may laugh or play at a time that appears inappropriate to an adult.

Talk about Death with the Child

Children need to feel that it is okay to talk about death and how they are feeling. If a child does not want to talk about his or her grief, adults need to respect that. Adults should let the grieving child know that they are available to listen and help and that any feelings the child has—anger, sadness, fear or regret are normal.

Hugging and touching helps the grieving child feel secure in expressing emotions and also reassures the child that he or she is loved and will be cared for. If grieving children are ignored, they may suffer more from the sense of isolation than from the loss itself.

Parents must select their words with care when sharing their expectations of a grieving child. The following will suppress the grieving process and create unfair expectations. "Don't cry. You need to be strong. You're the man in the family now. Be a good girl. Your mommy needs your help now more than ever." To force a child into adulthood is the improper rite of passage.

It is important that adults not hide their own feelings of grief from a bereaved child. If they do, they teach the child that feelings are not okay. It is also true that grieving adults should not grieve profusely and at length in front of a child since it may frighten and worry the child.

Other Sources of Help

Religion is an important source of strength for many adults and children during the grief process. Children takes things literally, so explanations such as: "It is God's will, He knows what is best," will comfort only if the child has been taught about the "love and ways of God." It's important to inquire how the child perceives what is explained about the death. It is also important that children be allowed to express their religious and spiritual concerns.

Parents may be tempted to send children away when there is a loss, in an attempt to protect them from painful feelings or because it is difficult to care for them while grieving themselves. This should only be considered in extreme cases. During the grieving period, children find comfort by remaining in familiar surroundings and routines, and separation may increase their fears about the loss or the feeling of rejection.

Expressions of Sadness

Grieving children who are sad or depressed require a lot of support and attention so that they can express their feelings and work through them.

Ways to Express Their Feelings

- Ask the child to draw how they are feeling.
- They may draw or write about their favorite time with the deceased.
- Write about things they would like to do with the deceased if it were possible.
- Allow the child to talk about their feelings without interrupting. Repeating is okay.
- Encouraging the child to engage in physical activity.
- Ask the child to write letters to God, if they understand His role in our lives.

Expressions of Anger

It is sometimes easier for a child to feel mad than sad. Anger does need to be expressed. However, the grieving children must be taught how to express it in a constructive way. Unexpressed anger can get out of control, and cause a negative impact on those around him.

Instead of asking an angry child to "calm down," it may be more useful to allow him or her to dispel the anger in other ways, such as running, exercising, scribbling on paper, ripping paper, and singing.

Don't ask the child why are they angry until the intensity has decreased. Consider asking questions like, "How does your body tell you that you are becoming angry? What are you thinking about when you become angry?" Learning what triggers the anger usually helps to diminish the intensity; and gives the child a sense of control. Maintaining household rules and chores actually increases the sense of normalcy and security for a grieving child.

Expressions of Guilt and Regrets

Some children have regrets about negative aspects of the relationship with the deceased or regrets about things that did not happen or were not said prior to the death. Examples might be: "I was mad at my mom the day she died, I didn't have a chance to say goodbye, I didn't tell my mom I loved her, I was angry with my father because he traveled and never attended my games." Helping the child express their guilt or regret is the first step to overcoming it.

Expressions of Fear

It is important to help a fearful child identify what they are afraid of, and then to address the fear. Children who are fearful generally need reassurance that the fear will not last. It is also important that a parent or other significant adult spend time with the grieving child. The child need to know that they are loved. Different techniques should be used to address the cause of the fear. If it was a car accident, then it will be necessary to reassure the child that it was an accident and they will be safe to ride in the car again.

Expressions of Physical Complaints

When a grieving child routinely has physical complaints like headaches and stomachaches, it is helpful to ask what other feelings he or she may be having. They may not want to talk about their emotions, however, they may share their physical and emotional concerns.

Sometimes the physical complaints reflect those of the deceased, it may be helpful to talk with the child about why the death occurred. Depending on the age of the child a visit to the pediatrician may help the child understand that nothing is wrong. For an older child a trip to the cemetery may help, if they can talk to the deceased about their feelings.

Exercises of Relief

Write a letter to the deceased describing their feelings. Tie it to a helium balloon and release the balloon into the sky. If the final resting place is nearby, you may want to take the child there and leave the letter.

For younger children, help them make two puppets and draw the child's face on one, and the deceased person's face on the other. Now ask the child to tell the puppet about their regret.

Revisiting the Death of a Parent or Significant Adult

It is natural for the parent or significant adult to love their children, and children depend upon parents for survival and stability. The death of a parent or significant adult may be more heartbreaking if the death was sudden, or if the child lacks a solid replacement figure in their lives.

If a child express strong desires of being with their parent, it is usually a thought for the moment, and not considered suicidal. However, if the conversation is ongoing the child should be asked how they plan to do that.

It is normal for children to revisit the death of a parent or significant person throughout their lives. The visits will occur during special events such as a girls sixteenth birthday, graduation, career accomplishments, marriage or the birth of the first child. It may also happen at the death of the other parent.

Grieving the Death of a Parent

When a parent dies, many adult children begin to explore the meaning of their lives and examine the direction their lives are taking. Some make significant changes in their lives.

Helpful Tips in the Loss of a Parent

- Acknowledge the importance of the loss and allow yourself to grieve completely.
- Feelings of anger, uncertainty, guilt and shame are normal.

- Don't pressure yourself to get back to normal.
- Address any unfinished business with your deceased parent by writing a letter, talking with someone you trust, talking to Jesus about it, or seeking help from a grief professional.

- Create new family patterns, rituals and ceremonies.
- Prepare in advance for special holidays and anniversaries.

- Join a bereavement support group to share your feelings with others.
- Each year, acknowledge the anniversary of the death of your parent.

- Create a memorial tribute by donating to a charity in your parent's name, planting a tree, visiting the cemetery, making a memory book or whatever works for you.
- Take your friends and family up on their offers to help. Be specific about what you need.

- Learn to pamper yourself. Surround yourself with people who love you.
- Take comfort in knowing that the pain you feel after the loss of a parent should lessen with time.

Help for a Young Widow

Becoming a young widow is an experience that completely turns your life inside-out. Everything that once made sense, no longer does. The pain feels agonizing, and you are suddenly thrust into unfamiliar territory.

Even if your spouse died from an illness, and you knew that death was near, you are never mentally ready for this type of life-transforming loss. Aside from the grief, being a young widow can add an extra level of complication to the healing process. It can be very isolating to be a woman in today's society, who has lost her spouse before the age of 60. People don't know what to say, how to approach you, and you may feel like you don't fit in anywhere.

To move through the grief process in a healthy way, it is important to know that you are not alone. There are practical tools that can help you nurture yourself, honor your loss, and bring you comfort and strength. By making use of these tools, you can once again learn to live whole-heartedly, find new passions or reclaim existing ones, and rejoin your community with strength and purpose.

ADDING COMFORT TO YOUR NEW LIFE

Talk about Your Loss

It is incredibly therapeutic to talk about what you have just experienced. Losing your spouse is very traumatic, and it can take years to process your feelings and emotions surrounding the story of your loss. It can bring you great comfort to talk about your loved one and most importantly, remember who they were and what they brought into your life.

You may find that certain stories bring you great joy to share. This is a huge step towards healing. Make sure that you talk with someone who will compassionately support you. Seeing a professional counselor or coach, in addition to speaking with close family and friends who you trust, can be extremely helpful. For a believer, personal scriptural meditation time can be helpful.

Find a Support Group

Being a young widow can be very isolating. You may feel like you are the only one going through this type of loss. You may feel awkward in social situations, especially if many of your friends and family members have significant others and can't relate to your experience.

It is important to find a support group specifically for young widows. You can find support groups online, such as *www.SoulWidows.org*. Even if you are nervous about attending a group, try at least one or two meetings so that you know if the experience will be a good fit for you. You will quickly learn that you are not alone.

Practice Self-Care

When you are grieving, it is so easy to let go of your health. Grieving can cause aches and pains in the body and make it difficult to eat properly and stay hydrated. You may find yourself gravitating towards unhealthy habits. "Grief can make you feel like you have a perpetual flu."

It is important to nurture your body with activities, such as taking a bath with aromatherapy salts, getting a massage or doing self-massage, drinking lots of water, taking a walk, gentle exercise such as yoga, cooking healthy meals or having someone prepare them for you. When you take care of yourself physically, this also will affect your mental and emotional state. If you are having difficulty getting out of bed, ask a close friend or family member to help you in accomplishing these acts of self-care. You deserve it.

Grieve At Your Own Pace

In today's society, we are all about rushing and getting things accomplished as quickly as possible. However, grief is the opposite. Moving through the grief and healing process takes time. There is no specific start and end date. You must allow yourself time to process and work through your feelings.

Other people around you may not understand the pace at which you are moving, but remember this is your loss. Your life has been altered in every way, and you have the right to take things one step at a time.

So, don't be afraid to tell the person who doesn't understand why you aren't feeling better after three months, that you are still coping with your loss, and that all you need is their ongoing support and respect. Even though they may not understand, it is vital to give yourself the time and space to move through it in a way that feels right to you.

Honor Your Loved One's Memory

There are so many beautiful ways that you can honor your spouse. By creating an activity around holidays, anniversaries and birthdays, you will get to experience ways in which their spirit lives on. You may wish to still hold a celebration for them with friends and family on their birthday. Perhaps there is a favorite spot that you used to go together that you can visit on your anniversary.

Create a memory album that has pictures of your life together and special events. Even though these actions may evoke tears and sadness, they also may fill your heart with comfort and feelings of closeness. You may wish to wear your spouse's wedding ring around your neck or have it melded together with your own ring to create one. There are so many unique ways to honor them. This will not only keep them alive in your heart and mind, but also allow others the opportunity to talk about them and honor them as well. It can be extremely healing to hear the way others miss and remember your spouse, and it can bring about a strong sense of community and togetherness.

GRIEVING PROCESS AVOIDANCES

Don't Isolate Yourself

If you cut yourself off from the world, you will most likely end up sinking into depression and despair. You will need some personal time to process what you're going through, but don't become a hermit and never see the light of day. If you do this, you will end up getting stuck in your grief and feel even worse about your situation.

Don't Try to Get Over It

When you lose a loved one, you never actually get over it. If you have ever heard this, it is a myth. While it is possible to move through grief and progress forward with your life, getting over a loss suggests that you will never again feel sadness or longing for your spouse or that it will never impact you again. Do not pressure yourself into believing that you should eventually get to a point where you are over it, and you can simply move on, putting it behind you.

This is unrealistic, and you will end up wondering what is wrong with you and why you are not over this yet. You will always carry the love you had for your spouse in your heart and nothing or nobody can take that away. Give yourself permission to move forward, but don't worry about getting over it. It is a loss that has changed you forever, and it can transform you in incredible ways if you allow it to.

Don't Deny Your Grief

Grieving is a confused and complex process. There is nothing neat and pretty about it. You will experience a rollercoaster of emotions. Some days, you will feel like you are taking two steps forward, and other days, you will feel like you are taking ten steps backwards.

But whatever you do, don't try to stuff the grief away and ignore it. Listen to what you are feeling and allow it to guide you on what you need. If you feel like you are putting on a face for other people to protect them from your true feelings, you are often doing a disservice to both yourself and them.

Be honest with yourself and what you are feeling, and go from there. Grieving is normal and healthy. It is a part of loss, and it should be recognized, witnessed and honored. By listening to your emotions, you will give yourself the opportunity to grow and expand in new ways. It is a time to get to know yourself on a deeper level, and you may discover that you uncover new wisdom in the process. Perhaps this will be wisdom that you can pass on to others someday.

Don't Expect Others to Read Your Mind

It is important to speak up about your needs while you are grieving the loss of your spouse. Many of the people around you might think they know what you need or want, but they may end up angering you in the process of trying to help. Don't be afraid to be straightforward with them, even when it comes to what they should or should not say. This can save you many heartaches and headaches.

Unless they also have lost a spouse or partner, they will not be able to fully understand what you are feeling or going through. They may feel lost and unsure of what to do. It can help to give them some direction or simply ask them to sit and listen if they don't know what to say. You may lose some friendships in the process, but also gain new relationships with people who can truly sit with you and support you in your grief.

Don't Be Too Hard On Yourself

Grieving the loss of your spouse can make you realize how little control you have in the world. No matter how much you may have willed them to stay alive or wanted to protect them, you ultimately did not get to decide. There can be many feelings of guilt, anger, shame and blame that can arise as a result. You may find yourself thinking: "If only I had done this differently, if I could have been there sooner, I should have known," and the list goes on.

It is important to accept and recognize your limitations. You are only capable of so much, and you can only do your best in any situation. Holding on to guilt or shame will not change the situation or result in anything positive. Remind yourself of the things that you do have control over and that nobody can take away. Consider the love that you shared with your spouse, the ways that you can continue to love and honor them or the things that you can do now to make a difference.

Create a Peaceful Place through Prayer

Inner peace, quiet time, meditation and peace of mind are all phrases used to describe the kind place we would like to fill when there is a loss of a loved one or a life threating situations. Would you say the challenge is how does one unlock that peaceful place?

Most people are well aware of the need, and desire to make a change. However, the ongoing question is how to activate that place; and stay focused on the time set aside to do whatever is necessary to fill that space, thus overcoming the emptiness.

We must keep in mind that peace and joy is in us. Both were given to every believer when they received the Holy Spirit into their lives. With that thought in mind we are equipped to be over comers of daily situations. The key is how to pray the scriptures related to our lives. The Holy Scriptures are key to finding the support that we need, consider these verses in the New King James Version of the Bible.

Psalm 4:8: I will both lie down in peace, and sleep; For You alone, O Lord, make me dwell in safety.

Psalm 29:11: The Lord will give strength to His people; The Lord will bless His people with peace.

Isaiah 26:3 You will keep him in perfect peace, Whose mind is stayed on You, Because he trusts in You.

John 14:27 Peace I leave with you, My peace I give to you; not as the world gives do I give to you. Let not your heart be troubled, neither let it be afraid.

John 16:33 These things I have spoken to you, that in Me you may have peace.

Romans 15:13 Now may the God of hope fill you with all joy and peace in believing that you may abound in hope by the power of the Holy Spirit.

Now turn the written word into a prayer for our personal situation. Try this as an evening prayer:

Jesus, as I prepare to end another day that you have given me to do so in peace. You promised that I would lie down not only in peace but you would grant me sleep. I thank you for knowing that I am not alone and shall be safe in you. Psalm 4:8.

Dear God, I pray that my thoughts have been on you, knowing that you promised that I would have undisturbed inner peace if I mixed it with my trust in you alone. Isaiah 26:3.

When praying remember that you are talking with your Heavenly Father, and can come to Him in your own way. It is a conversation with someone that loves and cares about you personally. The more you read and apply the scriptures by faith, they will become a way of life, and your place of peace will feel natural and comforting.

"The Christian life is not a constant high.
I have my moments of deep discouragement.
I have to go to God in prayer with tears in my eyes, and say,
'O God, forgive me,' or 'Help me.'"
– Billy Graham

HOSPITALITY IN THE OLD AND NEW TESTAMENT

King Solomon recorded, "There is no new thing under the sun;" did you know that hospitality was one of those things. Let's look at some examples in the Bible.

So he lifted his eyes and looked, and behold, three men were standing by him; and when he saw them, he ran from the tent door to meet them, and bowed himself to the ground, and said, "My Lord, if I have now found favor in Your sight, do not pass on by Your servant," "Please let a little water be brought, and wash your feet and rest yourselves under the tree." "And I will bring a morsel of bread, that you may refresh your hearts." Genesis 18:2-5

...and loves the stranger, giving him food and clothing. Therefore love the stranger, for you were strangers in the land of Egypt. Deuteronomy 10:19

So he arose and went to Zarephath. And when he came to the gate of the city, indeed a widow was there gathering sticks. And he called to her and said, "Please bring me a little water in a cup that I may drink." And as she was going to get it, he called to her and said, "Please bring me a morsel of bread in your hand."

Then she said, "As the Lord your God lives, I do not have bread, only a handful of flour in a bin, and a little oil in a jar; and see, I am gathering a couple of sticks that I may go in and prepare it for myself and my son, that we may eat it , and die." And Elijah said to her, "Do not fear; go and do as you have said, but make me a small cake from it first, and bring it to me; and afterward make some for yourself and your son."

For thus says the Lord God of Israel; "The bin of flour shall not be used up, nor shall the jar of oil run dry, until the day the Lord sends rain on the earth." So she went away and did according to the word of Elijah; and she and he and her household ate for many days. I Kings17:10-15

For I was hungry and you gave Me food; I was thirsty and you gave Me drink; I was a stranger and you took Me in; I was naked and you clothed Me; I was sick and you visited Me; I was in prison and you came to Me. And the King will answer and say to them, Assuredly, I say to you, inasmuch as you did it to one of the least of these My brethren, you did it to Me. Matthew 25:35-36, 40

Whatever city you enter, and they receive you, eat such things as are set before you. Luke 10:8

...and breaking bread from house to house, they ate their food with gladness and simplicity of heart, Acts 2:46

"If you have judged me to be faithful to the Lord, come to my house and stay." Acts 16: 15

... given to hospitality. Romans 12:13

Let brotherly love continue. Do not forget to entertain strangers, for by so doing some have unwittingly entertained angels. Hebrews 13: 1-2

"The word 'hospitality' in the New Testament
comes from two Greek words.
The first word means 'love'
and the second word means 'stranger.'
It's a word that means to love strangers."
by Nancy Leigh Demoss

May the eyes of your Heart be enlightened while sharing your Love through daily deeds of Hospitality!

ACKNOWLEDGMENTS

Have you observed how many people appear to ignore or are not aware of the importance of hospitality in their daily lives? *"How to Show Kindness Through Hospitality"* should change that for those that desire to.

To the editors: Holly Gage, Paula Goodnight, Keith Singleton, and Richard Sunburg. Special thanks to Marcie Eiser for her expertise in creating a cover that speaks "hospitality" through the pineapple. Contact Marcie at peerlessprinting.com. Printing done by One Stop Print Soltuions, LLC (www.onestopprintsolutions.com).

To the members of the Middletown Area Christian Writers Group, Ohio for their critiques, prayers and love.

And thank you to my Church family at God's House of Praise and Worship for their prayers on behalf of this project. Also, thank you to the many others who helped in some special way behind the scene.

RESOURCES

The information in this book was made possible through the following:

Inspiration of the Holy Spirit through prayer and meditation by the Author.

The Holy Bibles (see copyright page)
King James Version (KJV)
New King James Version (NKJV)
English Standard Version (ESV)

Research and Observations
Hospitality Sharing Our Love by Helen Rogers
Common Sense for Everyday Living by Helen Rogers
Personal Experiences of Helen Rogers through Seasons Of Life

Websites *
Tipcalculator.net
FinalResources.com
ForCremationAndMemorials.com
MSN.com/Lifestyle
TripSavvy.com
*Some sites may no longer be available

ABOUT THE AUTHOR

Helen Rogers, author and teacher, has spoked for diverse professional, educational and Faith-Based organizations throughout the country for over 35 years. She is an energetic speaker with spiritual depth who exemplifies her message: "I can do all things through Christ who strengthens me" (Philippians 4:13NKJV). In all of her teachings, she presents a wealth of practical social skills and life principles with actual life applications, and well-timed touch of humor.

The lives of many are empowered through her workshops, individual sessions, daily living, and books, including **Hospitality Sharing Our Love, Family, Friends and Community**, a prelude to her latest book **How to Show Kindness Through Hospitality.** God's love fuels her spirit of giving. Helen refers to herself as one chosen to help others regardless of the season of life they are experiencing (see Ecclesiastics 3:1).

Her unselfish contributions to the Young Women Christian Association of Hamilton, Ohio, the Ohio District Council Christian Women Auxiliary, God's House of Praise and Worship, and various other organizations has allowed her to encourage others with hope beyond their present environments.

OTHER BOOKS BY THE AUTHOR

POLISHED AND PREPARED SERIES

Visit seasons-of-life.com for ordering information

For Just a Time as This
Published by Seasons Of Life © 2003

Inspirations: from the Heart
Published by AuthorHouse © 2006

Hospitality Sharing Our Love
Published by Seasons Of Life © 2010

Surviving: The UneXpected
Published by Seasons Of Life © 2010

Global Opportunities: My Space of Employment
Published by Seasons Of Life 2010; 2nd ed. ©, 2014

Impacting the World Through The WORD,
68 Inspirational Promises of God for this Generation
Published by Seasons Of Life © 2016

THE POTENTIAL OF THE ACORN

by Helen Rogers

Once I am planted in the soil and surrounded by caring elements, I become, many things too many people... watch my life:

In the executive suite, I'm the desk; I'm the covering on the pen set. I'm the coat rack, I'm the door, I'm the floor and the window framework.

In the kitchen, I'm the cabinets; In the dining room, I'm the table and the chairs. O' I'm the frame for the picture on the wall. In the day room, I'm the case for the awards on the bookshelf, and for the flag of the ones who sacrificed their life for my freedom.

On the cruise ship, I'm the helm, the deck, and desk in the cabin.

On the canvas, the artist's paintbrush gave me a face; now I'm a person.

To the weary traveler, I'm a refuge from the sun. To the birds, I'm a source of food. I'm a nest for their young and a lookout for the predator.

To the squirrel, I'm a meal, and when time has aged me, I'm a home for the little creatures.

I am flexible.

Yes, I'm the acorn in the sand, and we, like the acorn, must be flexible in our Creator's hand on matter how humble our beginnings.

From the cotton fields of Alabama to Career Training Institute to the United States Marine Corps to Corporate America to Unemployment to Life Coach, sharing life principles.

With the leading of my Creator and the help of caring people, I am surviving the storms of life and helping other acorns achieve in the sands of time.

To God be the glory!

The mighty oak was once a little nut that stood its ground — the root of the righteous shall not be moved. (Proverbs 12:3)